Polymer Clay
Creative Traditions

Judy Belcher

Polymer Clay
Creative Traditions
TECHNIQUES AND PROJECTS INSPIRED BY THE FINE AND DECORATIVE ARTS

Principal Photography by
Steve Payne

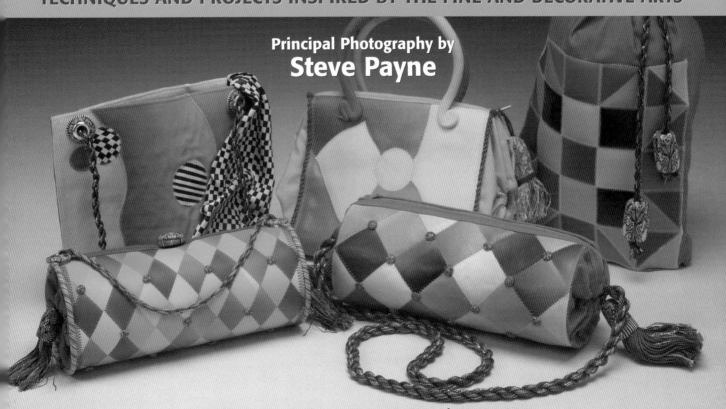

WATSON-GUPTILL PUBLICATIONS / NEW YORK

FRONTISPIECE AND TITLE SPREAD
Various polymer clay works by Judy Belcher

Senior Acqusitions Editor, Joy Aquilino
Project Editor, Robbie Capp
Designer, Areta Buk
Graphic Production, Ellen Greene
Text set in 10.75 Adobe Caslon

Unless otherwise identified, all photography by Steve Payne

First published in 2006 by
Watson-Guptill Publications,
a division of VNU Business Media, Inc.
770 Broadway, New York, NY 10003
www.wgpub.com

Library of Congress Control Number 2005927912
ISBN: 0-8230-4065-8

Printed in China

First printing 2006

1 2 3 4 5 6 7 8 9 / 14 13 12 11 10 09 08 07 06

FOR MARIA, MAX, AND GREG WITH MUCH LOVE.

ACKNOWLEDGMENTS

I would like to thank my parents, who have always encouraged my artistic curiosity and been so very supportive throughout my life, and my sisters and brother, who have been my biggest cheerleaders.

Great big thanks to Steve Payne, who was patient and funny, took amazing photographs, and sang great songs.

Thank you to Joy Aquilino, the senior acquisitions editor at Watson-Guptill who believed in this book, to Robbie Capp, project editor, who made me sound better than I could have hoped, and to Areta Buk for her beautiful book design.

My deepest appreciation to all the artists who contributed their wonderful artwork and extraordinary stories that make this book so interesting. Leslie Blackford gets special thanks for lending her time and wonderful talent to the sculpture chapter. Polymer clay has forged friendships that I value so much. Donna Kato has been a source of inspiration and generosity that I will always hold near to my heart. For their support, encouragement, wisdom, and laughs I thank Gail, Kim, Cathy, Sue, Jacqueline, Lisa, Olivia, Sandra, Marcia, Stephanie, and Amy.

I could not have written this book without the patience and cooperation of my wonderful husband, Greg, and my two creative and understanding children, Maria and Max.

ABOUT THE AUTHOR

Judy Belcher is based in St. Albans, West Virginia, where she is the president and a founding member of the Kanawha Valley Polymer Clay Guild and a member of the National Polymer Clay Guild. Her polymer clay work has been included in juried exhibitions and has been featured in several magazines and books. She has also demonstrated her varied techniques at trade shows, retail venues, and schools as well as on television, most notably on HGTV's *The Carol Duvall Show.*

ABOUT THE PRINCIPAL PHOTOGRAPHER

Steve Payne, whose company, Steve Payne Photography, is located in Charleston, West Virginia, is best known for his portraiture and fine-art landscape and nature photography.

CONTENTS

Our Most Versatile Art Medium

THE AIM OF THIS BOOK is to explore various art forms and show how they have influenced polymer clay artists working in many different disciplines. A glance at the "Contents" page shows the broad range of step-by-step demonstrations that lie ahead in chapters sequenced by art traditions based on glass, metal, fiber, painting/drawing, stone/bone/wood, and sculpture/ceramics. Polymer clay is the only medium that can emulate all of those different art forms, and more. It can be matte or shiny, rough or smooth, and can be formed into shapes and adornments limited only by the artist's imagination. It is that extraordinary versatility of polymer clay that prompted me to write this book.

Some of the art pieces shown are based on the traditional techniques that they emulate, step by step, and look very much like the art form they intend to replicate; others adapt certain techniques from a particular art form, but do not replicate its overall look. The distinctions between those categories will become clear as you progress through these pages, exploring diverse projects of my own creation and those of dozens of other artists who have graciously allowed me to include their work in this book. Many of them came to polymer clay from backgrounds that did not include academic training in the arts. I attribute their imaginative work with polymer clay to that very fact—that they were not bound by preconceived rules governing so many applied arts, but instead, let their own exploration of the medium guide their work with it, each bringing his or her own life experiences and visions to their art.

In fact, I myself am not classically trained in art; my background is in finance and accounting. But I have always loved art. My father was a university professor, so every summer we spent on the road, visiting historic sights, museums, and art galleries as part of my parents' plan to ensure that my sisters, brother, and I were exposed to fine arts and crafts. As a child,

I was drawn to art of all kinds. Once a week, I went to a neighbor's house after school to work in pastels, and I still remember how I loved to blend the colors, and how soft the medium felt. I started working with pen and ink as a teenager, under the guidance of a wonderful high-school art teacher who illustrated children's books. In college, although I was practical and majored in finance, I always chose art classes for all of my electives. My fascination with all art forms continued after college, especially my interest in working with clay, which I explored in several night courses in ceramics. I love the feel of clay in my hands—and, as all potters know, how gratifying it is to throw it on a wheel and create something unique. But I had to quit after I became pregnant with my first child, because I could no longer fit behind the wheel! Then I found the solution.

When I came upon art created with polymer clay, I learned that it not only didn't require working with a wheel and having access to a kiln, but also how versatile a medium it is. The first time I saw reproductions of the art form in Barbara McGuire's book *Foundations in Polymer Clay Design*, my response was, "Wow, you can do that?" My next book purchase was Donna Kato's *The Art of Polymer Clay*, and I declared, "Yes, I can do that!" As I began working with the medium, I discovered conferences devoted to it, and learned a lot from many of their participants. The sharing spirit of people who work with polymer clay astounded me.

My commitment to polymer clay has transformed my life and ushered in a rewarding new career, which eventually led to undertaking this book. It is my hope that it will offer fresh insights into working with polymer clay and encourage you, the reader drawn to this book, to take the techniques found here and, combined with your own imprint to make your art unique, you will reap personal satisfaction and creative fulfillment through the pleasures offered by working with polymer clay.

LORIE FOLLETT
Opal Tail Mermaid has golden fiber tresses and other mixed-media embellishments to complement her beautifully sculpted form. The artist is the winner of Donna Kato's 2004 exhibition "Feet of Clay."
PHOTO BY ARTIST

The History of Polymer Clay

EVEN THOUGH most of the artwork in this book is by artists residing in the United States, the history of polymer clay begins in Germany. The origins of the material now known as FIMO date back to 1939, when the famous German doll manufacturer Kathe Kruse was seeking a modeling compound that would be suitable to produce the doll's head. An oven-hardening material was given to her, but it did not meet with the high standards that Kruse had set for her work. However, her daughter, Sophie Rehbinder-Kruse, was fascinated by the claylike material and proceeded to create vases, tiles, mosaics, figurines, and toys with it. She also found practical and mundane applications for the compound, one such use being to make or repair the soles of sandals, which could then be bartered for bread and coal during the hard years following World War II.

When Rehbinder-Kruse went public with the modeling clay in 1954, she marketed the oven-kneading material in a few different colors under the name FIMOIK, an acronym combining letters from her nickname, Fifi, and the word *mosaic*, a popular art form at the time. FIMOIK was sold successfully to children, Rehbinder-Kruse's objective being to have every child in the world experience the joy of creating plastic forms.

In 1964, Eberhard Faber bought the rights to the modeling clay, improved its formulation—a mixture of polyvinyl chloride (PVC), plasticizer, and pigment—changed the brand name to FIMO, and began distributing it around the world. In 1974, Accent Import brought FIMO to the United States in a wide variety of colors. The owners of Accent Import, Ralf and Karinheide Schaup, both originally from Germany, had recognized FIMO's commercial potential when it was sent to them as a Christmas gift from abroad. They introduced the brand to American retailers by selling it from the back of their car. Other importers soon followed suit, and FIMO's distribution network broadened to include Dee's Delights in the 1970s and American Art Clay Company (AMACO) in the 1980s. FIMO is now available to consumers from coast to coast.

Through the years, other forms of polymer clay also came into being. In the 1960s, a product known generically as *polyform* was developed for industrial use, but when it didn't suit the purpose for which it was intended, the material was shelved—until a visitor to the company obtained a little batch of it, created a small figure from it, and baked it in a lab oven. That material was eventually sold as Sculpey, beginning in 1967. By 1976, Mike Solos, the company founder, was marketing Sculpey at craft shows and small retail shops. Until 1984, when Sculpey was produced in colors, artists such as sisters Sue Kelsey and Cathy Johnston used ground chalk and tempera powders to color their white clay.

Many other forms of polymer clay are on the market today, as reviewed in the "Materials" chapter that follows.

LAURIE MIKA
Tolerance: Polymer clay mosaic wall icon. PHOTO BY MIKE CAMPOS

Clays, Tools, Supplies

POLYMER CLAY is available at local arts-and-crafts stores and through catalog and Internet outlets. Superbly versatile, it can be sculpted, molded, carved, drilled, stitched—and much more. Although you need only your hands and a heat source to complete polymer clay projects, many special tools are helpful aids. But first, let's discuss the clay itself and how it is generally prepared for a project.

CLAYS

Soft and pliable until baked in a conventional oven, all forms and brands of polymer clay must be conditioned to distribute their ingredients evenly, ensure their strength, and make them pliable and easy to mold and shape.

Conditioning

To condition polymer clay, simply roll and twist it with your hands or use a pasta machine, to flatten and fold it. To tell if your clay is conditioned enough, fold a sheet of it in half. If there are cracks along the edge, it needs more conditioning. Be careful not to trap air in polymer clay. While air pockets may not be visible initially, they will appear as a raised area or result in a crack or hole after baking.

Storing, Baking

Store polymer clay in a cool area and out of direct sunlight. Then, after forming it into your art piece, place it on a clay-dedicated cookie sheet or ceramic tile and bake it in a conventional oven, toaster oven, or convection oven.

The baking temperatures and times included in this book's demonstrations are for Kato Polyclay; if you use any other brand, follow the manufacturer's recommended baking temperatures and times. Although all polymer clays have safety regulations printed on their packages, if you're worried about fumes or residue in your oven, place a roasting pan over the item.

Clay Brands

There are many brands of polymer clay. Each has its own characteristics that make it the particular choice of the artists whose works appear in this book. All of their projects, and mine, are based on the most updated forms and colors of polymer clay offered.

I choose Kato Polyclay for its superior strength and ease of conditioning and color blending. It does not become sticky, making it easy to mold and

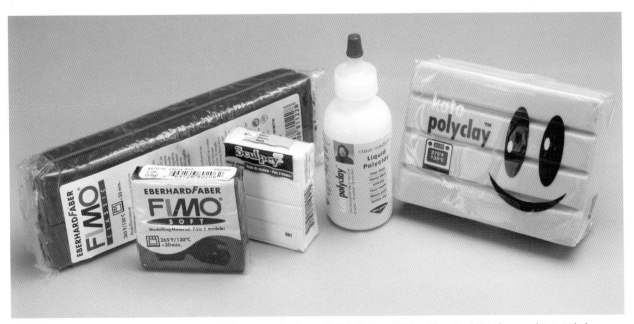

Popular brands of polymer clay include (from left) FIMO Classic, FIMO Soft, Sculpey III, Kato Clear Liquid Medium, and Kato Polyclay, which comes vacuum packed, keeping air from invading the clay.

texture. It holds even minute details clearly during the caning process, and firms up quickly for no distortion when the cane is sliced. Caning, a process that occurs frequently in these pages, is the technique that simulates millefiori, the ornamental glass form produced by cutting cross sections of fused bundles of glass rods of various colors and sizes.

For her amazing canework, Sandra McCaw chooses FIMO Classic polymer clay, which allows the intricate details of her subtle blends to remain sharp. While FIMO can be difficult to condition, she uses a food processor to help condition the clay and custom blend the colors she needs.

Jeff Dever finds Sculpey III polymer clay easy to condition. It retains its rigidity and brittleness when baked, keeping the fragile appendages and arcs that distinguish his designs from slumping or bending over time.

Pier Voulkos uses Premo! Sculpey for her art pieces, which contain great infusions of mica particles in the clay. She laminates the flexible baked sheets to her husband's wooden boxes.

Three major manufacturers of polymer clay have also developed their brands in liquid form. Translucent Liquid Sculpey comes in a variety of colors and has a thicker consistency than the other liquid clays. FIMO Liquid Decorating Gel is a bit thinner, but much more translucent. Kato Liquid Polyclay Clear Medium has the thinnest consistency and is also very translucent.

TOOLS

A **pasta machine** will not only aid in the conditioning of polymer clay; it also forms flat, even sheets of clay in a variety of thicknesses.

An **acrylic rod** or **brayer** can be used to form sheets, add texture, smooth surfaces, and aid in reducing canes.

A **sharp blade** such as the Kato NuBlade is for slicing; use a flexible tissue blade to cut curves and make thin slices; choose a craft knife for more intricate trimming and detailing. I love the slicing tool Precise-a-Slice made by Valkat Designs. It's incrementally marked and aids in making evenly cut beads and slices. It also has a 45-degree side that allows me to make precise cuts in canes when combining them.

Keep a **measuring tool** handy at all times. Remember the old woodworker's adage: "Measure twice, cut once." It's a great tip! I use a ruler or Marxit for spacing the slices of a cane and marking off sheets of clay to form precise, even beads.

Other tools that I find invaluable include a **drill** mounted to a drill press and various shaped wooden blocks to use as jigs for drilling holes precisely in beads. If you would like your polymer clay art to have a high-gloss finish, use wet/dry automotive **sandpaper** (800 to 1500 grit) or sanding sponges, and then buff with a single-stitched muslin **buffing wheel**.

A **heat gun** can be used to cure raw clay or set liquid clay medium. Quick-drying cyanoacrylate glue is helpful for adding pin backs or for holding pieces in place prior to baking.

Useful tools for preparing polymer clay include a pasta machine, Marxit (to mark clay for slicing and forming beads), ruler, craft knife, clay blade, brayer, and acrylic rod.

SUPPLIES FOR SPECIFIC ART FORMS

The supplies shown below are either borrowed from a specific art form or used to replicate a technique in that art tradition, as separated by chapters in this book. In addition to the following, each demonstration in this book opens with a "Supplies" box, where other items, specific to that demo, may be listed.

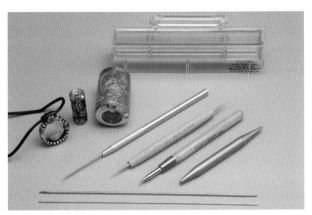

GLASS (from left): Reverse magnifying lenses to see how cane looks reduced. Foreground, thin knitting needles for holding beads. Behind them, (from left) a long needle tool; double-ended ball stylus; piercing tool; and double-ended knitting needle. Rear, roller for shaping various beads.

METAL (from left): metal powders in a variety of finishes; liquid that replicates a metal patina when applied to polymer clay; gold leafing; and a texture sheet.

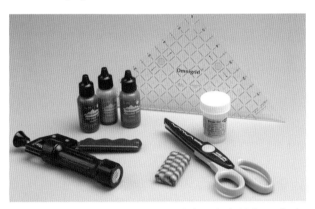

FIBER (from left): clay gun for strings of clay; alcohol inks; quilter's triangle; covered magnet; decorative scissors; and Repel Gel.

PAINTING AND DRAWING (from left): assortment of paints; pigment powders; and paintbrushes.

STONE, BONE, WOOD (from left): rubber stamp; manufactured mold; makeup brush for dusting powder as a mold release; water spritzer for mold release; two-part molding compound; and various embossing powders.

SCULPTURE (from left): rear, texture sheet and handmade texture rollers; center, sculpting and carving tools and cutters, including (right) dental tools; cutters of various shapes; and foreground, handmade stamps made of polymer clay.

1

GLASS
Traditions

Imagine that a Phoenician ship filled with a chemical compound to be used for embalming was on a trade route and stopped along a riverbank for the crew to prepare their meal. Without stones to support their cooking pots, they improvised by placing lumps of the soda compound into a fire built on the sands of the river. The result of this chance happening, as legend has it, was glass.

Legend aside, the actual time frame for the formulation of glass by mingling sand, soda, and lime with heat was likely to have occurred more than two thousand years earlier, since the first known examples of glass date back to the ancient Egyptians. Then later, it was the Romans who really took the art form to a much higher level, contributing many innovative techniques to the manufacture and decoration of glass items. One of the most important advances attributed to the Romans was the use of a hollow metal tube to blow air into the glass. This allowed not only for mass production of items such as goblets and vessels, making such articles affordable to the common man, but also led to many inventive decorative techniques.

When the art form spread throughout Europe over subsequent centuries, Venice, Bohemia, France, and England, in turn, became noted for further innovations, producing the special kinds of glass that became associated with each region. Polymer clay borrows so many of its rich techniques from the inventiveness of all those early glass pioneers—particularly the magnificent work created by Venetian glasswork artisans.

MAGGIE MAGGIO
Folk Art Beads inspired by Russian lacquer and Ukrainian eggs are made of polymer clay, using the millefiori technique. PHOTO BY BILL BACHUBER

PIER VOULKOS
These twelve imaginative polymer clay designs, displaying multiple techniques, were created for an international bead conference. PHOTO BY GEORGE POST

DIANE VILLANO
From her *Big Bead* series, the artist replicates African trade beads using the millefiori technique. PHOTO BY HAROLD SHAPIRO

SARAH NELSON SHRIVER
Taking up to a month to build a single cane, this artist then kaleidoscopes it into the many variations shown in this millefiori jewelry. But even before touching the clay, she gives much time and thought to color relationships, tonal values, and textural aspects of her patterns, all considered in detailed colored drawings before she builds a cane. PHOTOS BY GEORGE POST

FLAME, or *lampwork,* is the term for the technique of using a single heat source to melt and shape glass. The original source of the flame was an oil or paraffin lamp used with foot-powered bellows. Lampwork beads can be drawn or wound. A drawn bead is formed with a bubble inside the molten glass, which is then stretched into a tube and cut into smaller sections, each a bead. The Venetians were known for the wound method of lampworking, based on a metal rod and heating of the glass with a torch to form the bead. Many layers of decorative glass can be added and the bead may be reshaped during this process. Venetian lampwork was generally used for trade beads, which are now coveted as valued collectibles.

Polymer clay artists use many of the following decorative lampwork techniques to embellish a core bead.

MILLEFIORI

One of my first experiences with polymer clay came when I read an article about Sarah Nelson Shriver's amazing canework based on the millefiori technique. I was fascinated with the word *millefiori* and spent almost as much time researching its origins as I did building my first cane. Millefiori, which means "thousand flowers" in Italian, is the process of merging rods of glass into specific patterns, such as floral petals, heating the rods, and then stretching them out to form what is called the cane. The cane can be sliced and combined to simulate intricate floral and similar patterns, and then used to decorate beads or other glass objects.

The artisans of Murano, an island in the lagoon of Venice, led the decorative glass movement for more than five hundred years, and continue the art form to this day. Glass production was originally moved to Murano not only to safeguard the city from fire, but also to isolate the glass manufacturers and keep their time-honored methods a secret from the rest of the world.

Millefiori canework lends itself very well to polymer clay, and has gained wide popularity as an art form in the United States. The cane is formed by piecing the clay together like a puzzle, carefully compressing the outside to reduce the image. The resulting cane can be sliced to form beads or used as a decorative layer for other objects.

This Murano glass millefiori pendant was purchased for me by my parents on a recent trip to Italy. Its colors and symmetrical pattern are characteristic of the classic Venetian art form.

Artists' Networking Develops Millefiori Canework Across the United States

When did this colorful art form gain such wide popularity in America? In questioning many people, I found that all roads began with artist Pier Voulkos, who was in New York working as a dancer when she began to create jewelry made of shrink plastic. Looking for a bead accent for her creations, she experimented with a modeling compound she had purchased in Germany, and found it far more interesting than shrink plastic. That unusual compound was, of course, polymer clay, and Pier soon switched to it for all her jewelry pieces. Added to her fine-art knowledge and degree in ceramics, the versatile artist drew inspiration from the inlay work of Jane Piezer, her ceramics mentor. She also found ideas in—of all things—candy design. Thus, millefiori using polymer clay was born.

Pier's dance career then led her to Jennie Breene, who was also a New York dancer, and her sister, Martha. When Martha saw Pier's work, she began making her own remarkable polymer clay millefiori creations, retailed under the name Urban Tribe. Martha also spent many afternoons discussing millefiori caning with artists Michael and Ruth Ann Grove. They, in turn, produced their creations under the brand

PIER VOULKOS
Water/Wave: A polymer clay neckpiece takes on added dimension with its red accents interspersed among the gentle sea-blue-and-white overlapping shapes. PHOTO BY GEORGE POST

name "It"—then moved to one-of-a-kind sculptural pieces labeled "Grove and Grove." Their prolific output was featured in many exhibitions and publications.

Meanwhile, Martha Breene's mother, no doubt the recipient of many of her daughter's works of art, was a neighbor of Steven Ford, who with his partner, David Forlano, began CityZen Cane, specializing in intricate canework that propelled them into the national spotlight in fine-art circles. Pier's work also found its upscale following when it began being carried by Julie Shaffer Dale's fine-art gallery, Julie Artisans on Madison Avenue in New York. It was there that Helen Baines purchased one of Pier's necklaces and took it to the Torpedo Factory in Alexandria, Virginia, where she showed her treasure to Nan Roche, Kathy Amt, and Kathleen Dustin, who all recognized the added excitement that canework could bring to their already illustrious art careers.

Obviously, the chain of artists who find inspiration in millefiori canework doesn't stop there. As more—including you—work with it, its continued growth and development as a fine-art form is assured.

Thank You, Judith Skinner

I could not have been more excited upon learning that my roommate at a Colorado retreat would be none other than the eminent polymer clay artist Judith Skinner. The technique she developed for making polymer clay color gradients is indispensable to the medium and bears her name. "Skinner Blend" is the term we use in our home to describe anything that has a gradation of color. (My son once commented that his cousin had "Skinner Blend legs" after returning from a day at the beach.) When I told my daughter who my roommate was going to be she said, "Mom, how will you sleep with all the glow from her bed?" Little did we know just how true that tongue-in-cheek statement was. Judith likes to take computer books to bed with her and there was, literally, often a glow from her bed's nightlight.

Eager to know how Judith devised her famous blending technique, when I posed the question, she related her story to me, with permission to share it with you. "I discovered my artistic side," she began, "under my high-tech veneer after the age of forty, when I took some classes in interior architecture at UCLA." At that time, working as a software-system engineer, Judith had thought about changing careers. She knew she could master the technical parts of design work, but thought

she might need help with its creative aspects, so she took some design courses. "Then I purchased Nan Roche's book *The New Clay*", Judith continued, "and several colors of FIMO, and began to work, combining my technical side with my newly found artistic side. As I wear very little jewelry, I began by making a badge cover to wear with my picture ID for my job with NASA's Jet Propulsion Laboratory. I especially liked appliqué, or onlays, but wanted a background more interesting than a solid color. Why not try a simple color gradation?" she thought.

Although she had seen the beautiful work done by CityZen Cane using step blends, Judith couldn't imagine using a step blend for an area as small as her badge cover, so she resolved to design a new process. After developing and testing her method by making more blends for her badge covers, she wrote it up on her Website and posted it to the Internet.

By the time of Ravensdale—a large polymer clay teaching conference a few months later—Judith noted that "everyone was doing it. Kathleen Dustin and Nan Roche insisted the technique be given a name, my name, and so it was anointed the 'Skinner Blend.' I am still amazed to hear my name on television and see it in books," she concluded with delight.

JUDITH SKINNER
A necklace of nestling leaf forms that have soft, subtle blends of color characterizes the exquisite work of the polymer clay artist whose innovative blending technique bears her name.

SUPPLIES
polymer clay in two colors
pasta machine

DEMONSTRATION # Skinner Blend

When I demonstrate the Skinner Blend in a public setting, the look of amazement on viewers' faces and the sheer joy of children as they turn the pasta machine crank to help me make the blended magic always draws crowds around my table. The technique is incorporated in almost every piece of work that I do, and is used in projects throughout this book. At its simplest, a Skinner Blend works with any two colors of clay. After you've practiced with two, try multicolored blends. As you follow the demo steps below, although the sheets pictured have nice blended lines, don't panic if yours does not. Only with experience—when you fold the clay exactly the same way each time it goes through the pasta roller, then trim off the excess clay—will that occur. So, if clay isn't well blended, streaks may result. Also note that a blended sheet rarely remains rectangular. It will also move to the full width of the pasta machine if not forced to remain the same width. (This will be discussed further, when you get to the chapter on fiber.) So, if you ever see this method demonstrated on television and wonder why your blended sheet is not a nice neat rectangle, it's because the pro demonstrating it has folded and trimmed the clay meticulously.

❶ Begin with two right-angle triangles, joined on the diagonal, to form a rectangle of clay. If you try this demo with colors other than the two shown here, to be sure that they will be pleasing when mixed together, pretest by blending two little balls of clay in your choice of colors to see what occurs in the central part of the blend.

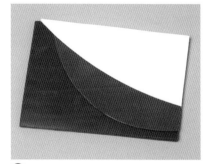

❷ Fold the two-color sheet in half, folding same color edge on same color edge. With the folded edge against the rollers of the pasta machine, roll it through. Be sure to keep the folded edge against the rollers so as not to trap air in the clay.

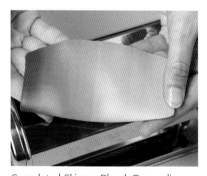

❸ Continue folding the clay in half and rolling through the pasta machine. Check each and every time that you are folding the same way and that the colors on each edge are the same. You will begin to see the blending after only a few passes through the machine.

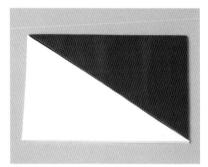

❹ Make sure you fold the clay in half exactly the same way each time you roll it through the pasta machine and your blend will be perfect.

❺ A multi-colored Skinner Blend can be achieved by combining several colors of clay. Try bending the blade to create curves of the colored sheets. Pay attention to what colors are more saturated and will overpower other colors.

Completed Skinner Blend: Depending on your pasta machine's setting, a blended sheet usually occurs with 20 to 25 passes, producing this beautiful, seamless gradation of colors.

SUPPLIES
black polymer clay
white polymer clay
sharp blade
acrylic rod
pasta machine
Marxit
mirror

DEMONSTRATION Two-Color Tessellation

While this finished millefiori canework looks quite intricate, each component is just a basic cane in itself. The word *tessellation* comes from the root *tesserae*, the little tiles used in mosaic work to form variegated patterns. The term applies well to polymer clay canes. Using two Skinner Blend "jellyrolls," a striped jellyroll cane, and a checkerboard cane formed into a right triangle, a series of complex-looking square canes can be created. Because a polymer clay cane can be manipulated, the right triangle (triangle having a right angle) can be reshaped into an equilateral triangle (having three equal sides), and many circular canes may also be formed. The dilemma you may have with this canework will be deciding which combination to choose to form your final canes.

1 Roll out two sheets each of conditioned black and white clay on a pasta machine at the #1 setting. Cut a 3"-x-4" rectangle of each color. On each, mark 1" in at the top and ³/₄" up from the bottom right edge. Cut each rectangle diagonally into two sections, from mark to mark. Recombine the rectangles, replacing the top right black triangle with the same size white triangle, and vice versa with the remaining triangles.

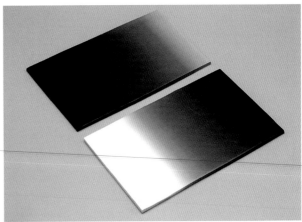

2 After employing the Skinner Blend (see page 19), the result will be two blended sheets of clay, one lighter in value, the other darker. Notice the contrast in the two sheets by the adjustment of the cut of the original rectangles.

3 Cut each blended sheet in half and stack to form a double thickness, keeping like colors aligned. This results in two blended strips measuring 1¹/₂" × 5". Bevel the ends of each blended strip using an acrylic rod.

4 Roll out one sheet each of the white and black clay measuring 1¹/₂" × 9¹/₂" on the #6 setting on a pasta machine. Lay the thin sheet of white clay on the dark blend and adhere with an acrylic rod.

5 Form into a jellyroll, beginning with the darkest end. Repeat the process using the thin sheet of black clay on the lighter blend. Form the jellyroll beginning with the lightest end of the light blended strip. This will form two jellyrolls of varying values.

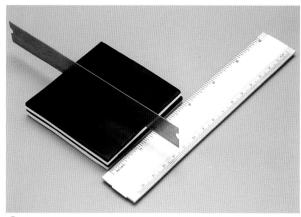

6 For the striped jellyroll cane, cut sheets of black and white clay into two rectangles, 6" × 3" each. Stack them and adhere with an acrylic rod. Cut in half, forming two squares of 3" × 3". Stack the squares to form a loaf of black and white stripes.

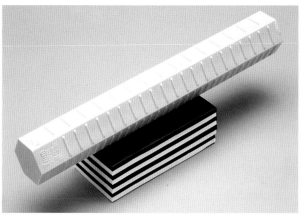

7 Repeat the process to end with a striped loaf that is 1 1/2" × 3", eight stripes high. Mark the loaf with a Marxit tool, using the 3mm side of the tool on the 3" length of the clay. Cut the loaf into about 22 segments.

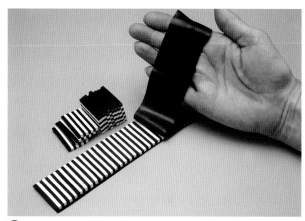

8 Roll out two sheets of black clay 1 1/2" × 9 1/2" on the #6 setting on a pasta machine. Lay out seven segments end to end, adhering each segment to one of the thin black sheets with an acrylic rod to form a sheet of black and white stripes. Adhere the second sheet of thin black clay to the top of the striped sheet.

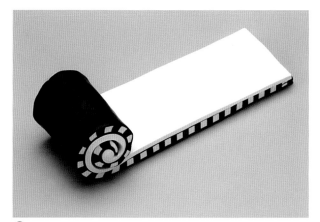

9 Roll out a white clay sheet of 1 1/2" × 6" on the #1 setting of a pasta machine. Adhere this sheet to the striped sheet using an acrylic rod. Form the jellyroll, leaving one inch from the end unrolled. Pack this area with any unused white clay sheets.

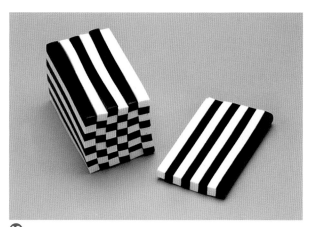

10 To form the checkerboard cane, use the remaining segments of striped clay (cut in Step 7). Flip over every other segment, making sure each black block aligns with the corresponding white block.

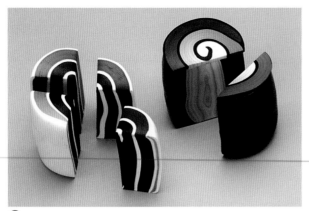
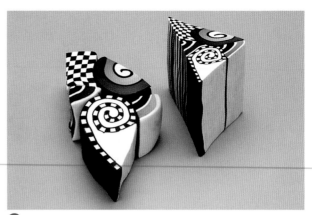

11 To assemble the final right-triangle cane, cut the dark jelly-roll in two pieces, one being a third of the cane, the other, two-thirds; the larger piece will be used in the right triangle. The lighter jellyroll is cut into quarters.

12 Place the striped jellyroll to the right, just below the two-thirds piece of dark jellyroll. Embed two of the quarters of lighter jelly-roll pieces into the cane. Add the checkerboard piece. If needed, fill in the rest of the right triangle with white clay.

13 Reduce the cane by pressing it against a tabletop, being careful to retain its original right-triangle shape. Stretch it to a length of 8" and cut into two pieces for the building of different finished canes. By cutting one of the segments in half and mir-roring the canes, a square is formed. Reduce to 8" and cut into four segments of equal lengths. Recombine, carefully mirroring each image. Each side of the square can be mirrored, so try all combinations to see which is most pleasing to you.

14 Compress the remaining segment into an equilateral trian-gle (having equal sides) and reduce to a length of 6", then cut into three equal pieces. Mirror each segment to form half a hexagon. By using a mirror, you can see what the finished circle will look like. Images 13 and 14 are slices from the cane. It is a good way to test all the combinations before committing to recombining a whole cane.

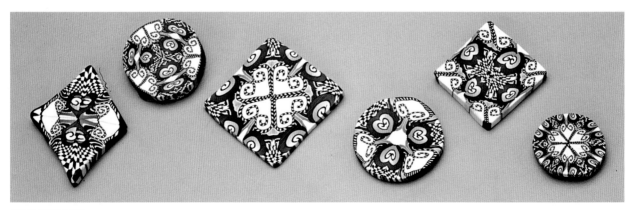

JUDY BELCHER
Completed Two-Color Tessellation Canework: Here are just a few of the endless combinations that can be created with this fun-filled technique. Use the cane slices for bracelet tiles or pendants; or combine several slices to adorn a box or light-switch cover. Bake as per the polymer clay manufacturer's instructions.

Encased Beads

SUPPLIES

polymer clays: white, ultra blue, green

thin knitting needle

coordinating pigment powders

melting pot

embossing powder

Gloss Flecto Varathane clear finish

blunt-ended tool (paintbrush handle)

In encased lampwork, a base bead of clear glass is formed around a mandrel (tapered spindle). By using glass rods in various colors, petals or other patterns are plunged beneath the surface of the molten glass bead. Patience and practice are required to perfect this technique; Debbie McComas is a glass artist who has mastered it. I challenged myself to replicate the look of one of her encased beads, using polymer clay. Although it will never have the translucence of glass, using an embossing powder as the encasing layer of the bead will produce the same visual depth.

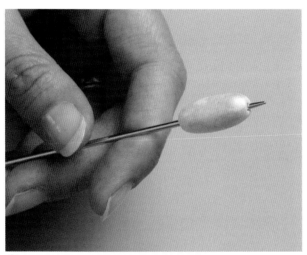

❶ Make a tube-shaped base bead of white clay. Add coordinating powders sparingly to lend interesting effects. Skewer the bead on a thin knitting needle.

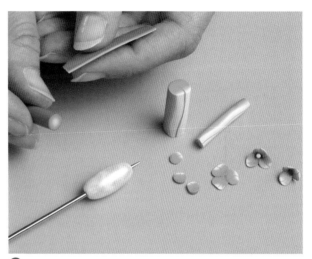

❷ Create small flower petals by rolling a very thin Skinner Blend sheet into a bull's-eye cane. For stems, use a green-to-white Skinner Blend bull's-eye cane, rolled flat to form a thin sheet with a light-colored center, dark outside. Slice each cane thinly to form flowers and stems.

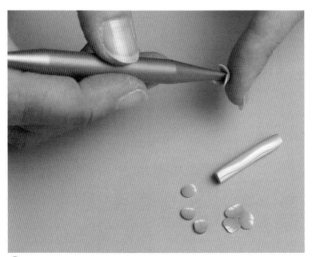

❸ Add the dimensional flowers and stems to the base polymer clay bead, embedding the center of the flower with a blunt-ended tool. Put a small stamen in the center of the flower. Bake for 30 minutes at 275 degrees; let it cool.

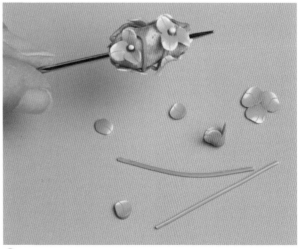

❹ Dip the bead, still attached to the knitting needle, into embossing powder (I use Ultra Thick by Ranger) that has been melted (I use Suze Weinberg's Melting Pot by Ranger; follow manufacturer's directions).

5 Hold the knitting needle horizontally and twirl it gently to adhere the embossing powder around the clay. Continue twirling until the liquid embossing powder becomes firm; it may take several dips into the liquid to achieve a rounded bead. The flowers will look as though they are submerged beneath a layer of glass.

6 Paint on a coat of clear gloss finish (I use Gloss Flecto Varathane) to keep the beads clean and free of fingerprints. The ends of the beads are sometimes irregularly shaped; using end caps will give them a more finished look.

JUDY BELCHER
Completed Encased Bead: How does my finished work (left) made of polymer clay compare with the encased glass bead (right) that inspired it?

TIP
If you are not satisfied with the bead, melt the embossing liquid with a heat gun over the melting pot and try again.

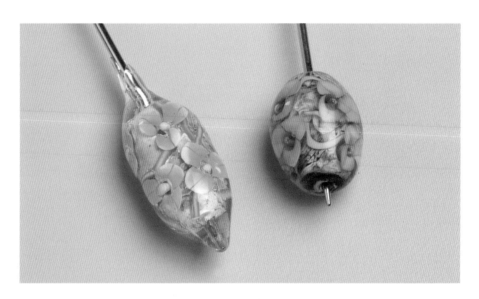

LIBBY MILLS
Drizzle Beads are by an artist who has won many awards for her replication of lampwork-style beads. Here, based on a subtle gradation of purple to blue to silvery tones, luminescence enhances these free-form polymer clay beads.

FIORATO

Fiorato lampwork beads are created using melted glass to "paint" three-dimensional flowers, swirls, and other decorations directly onto a base bead. Aventurine, a type of glass that incorporates metal oxides to form crystals, gives these beads a wonderful sparkle. This can be replicated in polymer clay, as evidenced by the work of Ann and Karen Mitchell shown here.

LEFT ANN AND KAREN MITCHELL, ANKARA DESIGNS
Commenting on their fiorato lampwork, this design team says, "There are quite a few advantages to making Venetian-style beads in polymer clay, instead of glass. No torches or dangerous equipment are required for the process, and the beads are less fragile." PHOTO BY AI BUANGSUWON

BELOW DAN ADAMS
A "Warring States" necklace by a noted glass bead maker and lecturer on the genre, who, interestingly, is the husband of polymer clay artist Cynthia Toops. PHOTO BY ROGER SCHREIBER

DEMONSTRATION # Chinese Eye Beads

Dating back as far as the fourth century B.C., during the Warring States period in Chinese history, eye beads have mysterious origins. Some scholars believe they were created domestically; others think they were brought into Asia along the silk-trade routes. Adding layer upon layer of glass dots, one atop another, forms the eyes, or horns, of the beads. The brands I used for this demo are listed—in addition to my usual Kato Polyclay and Kato clear liquid medium—but of course, other colors and comparable tools of your choice may be substituted.

1 Form a base bead of black polymer clay into rounded beads and flatten them with a slab of glass.

2 Pierce the beads with a knitting needle and bake for 20 minutes at 275 degrees.

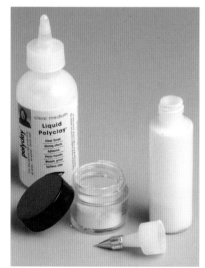

3 To color your liquid clay, add powdered pigments and mix thoroughly, using a ratio of $1/2$-oz liquid clay to $1/8$-tsp powder. Let the mixture rest until air bubbles rise to the surface and pop, then transfer the liquid to applicator bottles with fine metal tips.

4 While the beads are still hot, place a dot of white liquid on one side of each bead and rebake for 5 minutes. Use two wooden blocks with scrap clay balls to secure the knitting needle while baking. This keeps the beads off the baking pan but allows them to turn freely on the needle. Rotate the beads one-quarter turn after each 5-minute baking period, adding white liquid dots on all four sides. After each application, return beads to the oven immediately.

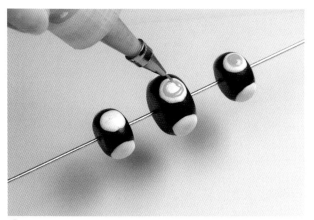

5 Repeat the process with the green liquid, making smaller dots on the white ones. Rotate the beads after each 5-minute baking period until all four sides are finished.

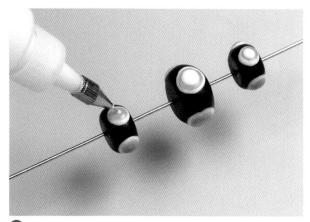

6 Repeat the process with the white liquid, making smaller dots on the green ones. Rotate the beads after each 5-minute baking period until all four sides are finished.

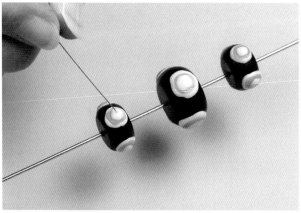

7 Use a fine pin to pop any air bubbles that may appear in the liquid clay before baking.

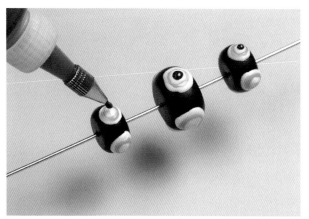

8 Repeat the process with the black liquid, making slightly smaller dots on top of the white ones. Rotate the beads after each 5-minute baking period until all four sides are finished.

JUDY BELCHER
Completed Chinese Eye Beads: A coat of gloss varnish will give them the appearance of glass. Here is the progression from plain black base to colorful beads.

MOSAICS

SMALL, TILELIKE PIECES formed into a pattern have a long history as a rich and distinctive way to decorate floors and walls. Particularly notable were fifth-century Byzantine mosaics made of thick sheets of colored glass, sometimes backed with silver or gold leaf to catch the light from all possible angles. Church patronage of the arts also produced centuries of mosaic works built around religious themes.

To simulate mosaics in polymer clay, some artists prebake their clay tiles, then join them by grouting with softened clay or liquid polymer clay. Others replicate mosaic work by using unbaked clay, then digging out the pattern from its surface.

ABOVE STEVEN FORD AND DAVID FORLANO
Mosaics, 11 × 4 × ¹/₄", is made of caned polymer clay, 1996. PHOTO BY ARTISTS

RIGHT AMY SEYMOUR
The polymer clay tiles for this work were prebaked, then assembled with softened clay grouting.

FUSED AND SLUMPED GLASS

FUSED GLASS combines sheet glass, crushed glass, and powdered glass to create designs, which are then fused in a kiln. The process can be taken an additional step by placing the glass over a mold, and as the glass melts, it slumps down and takes the shape of the mold. The works of James Lehman look so much like slumped glass, people are often surprised when he encourages them to lift one of his objects to see how light it is.

JAMES LEHMAN
This undulating polymer clay bowl was sanded, sanded, and sanded some more, then buffed and given several coats of lacquer to achieve its iridescent, glasslike shine. The reflection of the bowl, which was photographed on glass, is shown beneath the bowl.
PHOTO BY ARTIST

Glass Traditions in Polymer Clay

ABOVE KLEW (KAREN LEWIS)

Pendant Bead: Known as "Klew," this artist used a glass bead as the base for her stylized signature leaves made of polymer clay millefiori cane. The gold wire is cleverly run through the bead and looped at each end, allowing it to be worn as a pendant.

RIGHT JUDY BELCHER

Millefiori Jewelry: A pendant, bracelet, and pin are given a subtle, two-color palette, rather than multicolor—a good choice for coordinated jewelry pieces designed to be worn together.

MARLA FRANKENBERG
Sunflower Bowl: Layered millefiori in a subtle pastel palette is the result of careful blending of various polymer clay colors on this bowl. Millefiori flowers and leaves with translucent clay borders are applied to the interior of the bowl.

BOB PARIS AND NANCY BUNDY
Ladies: Millefiori cane slices add dimension to this pair of whimsical polymer clay earrings.

KIM KORRINGA
Beach Women: Polymer clay canes that appear to be mosaic tiles for their bodies, and glass accent beads strung on silver wire and wool cord for their hair, produce these playful figures.
PHOTO BY ARTIST

CYNTHIA TOOPS
The creator of this cuff bracelet amazed the polymer clay community with her micro mosaic work that uses tiny slices of hand-rolled threads of baked clay, as seen in this jewelry embellished with sterling silver. PHOTO BY ROGER SCHREIBER

BARBARA SPERLING
Blue Iris, a pendant strung on a beaded cord, blends the artist's love of nature and art with her wonderful perception of color, form, and design. PHOTO BY ROBERT DIAMANTE

CYNTHIA TINAPPLE
This artist uses a dual heat gun method to cure the mosaic polymer clay tiles she inlays in wood bowls crafted by her husband, Blair.

ABOVE EILEEN LORING
Zuni Bears combine abstract shapes with varied design motifs built into polymer clay canes and applied to a traditional earthen clay color.

RIGHT DIANE LUFTIG
Blossoms: Colorful flowers of polymer clay form this bold bracelet. PHOTO BY ARTIST

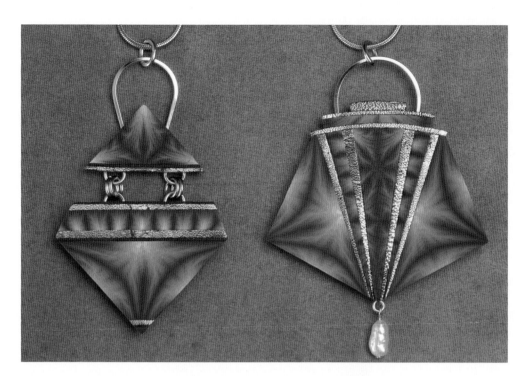

SANDRA MCCAW
Pendants: The precise cuts and angles in this millefiori cane took days to construct. The polymer clay pendants are adorned with 24k gold leaf and 14k gold wire.

CARLA JIMISON
Caravan: Graceful animals, inspired by Egyptian motifs, encircle this polymer clay necklace and bracelet set.

CONNIE DONALDSON
Heart: This wonderfully colored butterfly wall sculpture, based on millefiori cane, is approximately 8 × 6".

2

METAL
Traditions

Metallurgy is one of earth's oldest sciences and has had a significant impact on the art world. The discovery and development of metals can be traced as far back as 8000 B.C. Copper was beaten into tools and weapons by early man. Gold, whose scientific symbol is Au from the Latin *aurum,* meaning shining dawn, was used mostly for jewelry and ornaments, because the same malleability that allowed it to be formed easily also made it unsuitable for utilitarian objects. Pure silver, like gold, was used decoratively and as a measure of wealth.

Iron was also used as an adornment, both for the body and the home, and displayed as a symbol of great wealth, being five times more expensive to mine than gold. And owning aluminum, not known until the early nineteenth century, was also originally a sign of status. Napoleon III, it was alleged, reserved his aluminum utensils only for his most honored guests; all others were given mere gold and silver tableware.

When it was discovered that adding mica particles to certain clays could simulate the look of silver, gold, copper, and mixtures of all of these, many techniques used in metal art were transferred to polymer clay, producing the look of the metal itself. I've focused on the classic techniques of mokume gane and enamelware, with variations of each demonstrated. You will also see handsome examples of work by contemporary artists who have adapted these methods to their own unique polymer clay creations.

ANN DILLON
Wedding Necklace simulates a mokume gane assemblage of contrasting shapes in polymer clay. PHOTO BY ARTIST

MOKUME GANE (pronounced moKUmay GAmay) is a classic Japanese metalsmithing technique developed in the seventeenth century by Denbei Shoami, a master metalsmith. While searching for a way to strengthen samurai swords, he found that by laminating different metals, not only did he increase the strength of the sword, but also created an unusual layered pattern when forged and filed. This process cannot be cast or mass-produced; each piece must be hand-formed by fusing together thin layers of different metals. The piece is then carved, hammered, and filed to reveal its layers. This technique is sometimes called metal wood graining, as the patterns that form may look like a slice of a tree.

There are many other techniques in polymer clay that are also called mokume gane—any method that involves thin layers of clay that are manipulated in some way, then shaved off to reveal the pattern. Other artists have used paints, inks, powders, and inclusions such as spices and flower petals as the layers to be exposed.

The most authoritative, "must have" book about mokume gane is by Steve Midgett, of the metal-working studio Earthshine. Considered *the* American authority on the subject, Steve finds that using polymer clay is a quick and easy way to figure out patterns for his mokume jewelry designs. He says, "A new pattern that would take hours or days to laminate and pattern in metal can be easily constructed in polymer clay. When I teach workshops, I always recommend that students test new patterns that way. Because polymer clay exhibits the same, albeit softer, plastic qualities as metal, it clearly shows how carving and various manipulations will affect the metal laminate."

STEVE MIDGETT
Mokume Gane Shield Form Pins: Materials used include (left and right) 18k gold, palladium, silver, shakudo, copper, brass, diamonds, and rubies. The pod-form pendant (center) is made of 18k gold, shakudo, silver, copper, brass, and tsavorite garnet. The creator of these mokume gane pieces, an esteemed expert on the genre, usually works out his intricate jewelry design in polymer clay first, to see how the carving and various manipulations will affect the metal laminate. PHOTO BY RALPH GABRINER

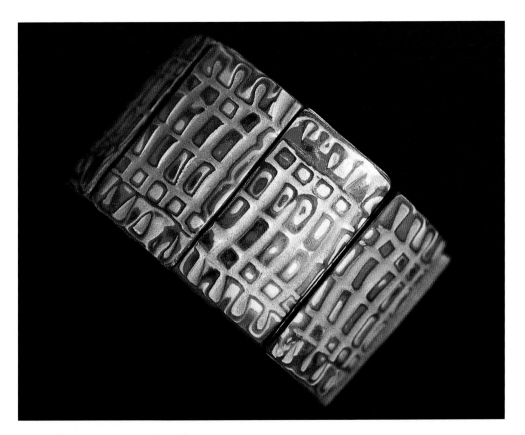

GWEN GIBSON
For this mokume gane bracelet, traditional techniques were employed, incorporating translucent polymer clay and gold leaf. PHOTO BY ROBERT DIAMANTE

TAMMY GARNER
Sparkling Necklace: This mokume gane polymer necklace owes its sparkling patina to the artist's choice of colors that imitate those of real gold, silver, and copper.

SUPPLIES

translucent polymer clay

pinches of three analogous colors

silver leafing

sharp blade

acrylic rod or brayer

blunt-ended tool (paintbrush handles)

DEMONSTRATION # Hills and Valleys

The first time I saw this mokume gane technique, it was demonstrated by my teacher, Lindly Haunani, who has been credited as one of its originators for use with polymer clay. Her steps mimic the ancient metal masters by layering thin sheets of analogous colors (those that fall next to each other on the color wheel) of translucent clay sandwiched between sheets of metal leaf. The colors shown and the kind of leafing may be substituted by your own choices.

① Condition six sheets of translucent clay and tint with small amounts of analogous colors, such as turquoise, violet, and magenta. Roll the clay out into thin sheets and trim into 2"-x-3" rectangles. Reserve the excess clay for a later step.

② Smooth a sheet of silver metal leafing (I use Old World Art Silver) with your finger to the top of each sheet. Continue to smooth until all the air is forced out from between the sheet of clay and the metal leaf.

③ Stack the sheets of clay, rolling each layer with an acrylic rod or brayer to ensure that there is no air trapped between the layers.

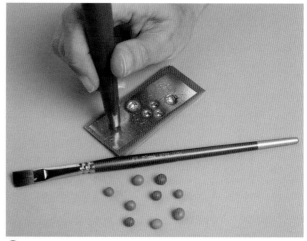

④ Using the excess clay from Step 1, roll various-size balls of each of the different colors of clay. Set them aside to firm up or put them in your freezer (but be sure to dry them off prior to use). With the blunt end of a paintbrush, make depressions in the clay stack and insert the balls into those cavities.

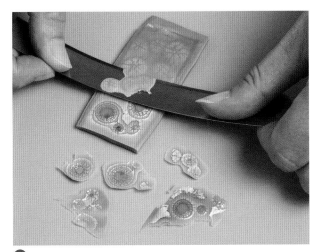

5 Turn the manipulated stack over and lay it flat on your work surface. With a sharp blade, such as this Kato NuBlade, cut thin slices randomly across the top of the stack to reveal the pattern. The slices removed from the top can also be used to decorate other sheets of clay. Wipe your blade after each pass; use alcohol or a baby wipe if minute pieces of leafing stick to the blade.

6 Use your brayer or acrylic rod to adhere and smooth those pieces onto additional sheets. Bake your finished piece as per the clay manufacturer's instructions.

TIP

The true depth of this mokume gane technique shines when the finished piece is sanded and polished. Use sandpaper (800 to 1500 grit) or a sanding sponge, then buff to a high sheen with a buffing wheel.

JUDY BELCHER

Completed Mokume Gane Hills and Valleys: Using translucent clay allows for many varied looks when the slices are applied to base sheets of assorted colors. Notice how different these three similarly styled pendants look by using violet (left), magenta (center), and turquoise (right) as the base sheet.

SUPPLIES
polymer clays, white,
turquoise, green
pasta machine
sharp blade
texturing sheet
water spritzer
acrylic rod
address book
pen
white glue

DEMONSTRATION # Texture Stamping

This variation on the basic mokume gane technique uses a texturing sheet or rubber stamp to impress images into the clay. I used Lisa Pavelka's rubber texture sheet "Swingin' Swirls," which is available on her website, but any deeply cut rubber stamp may be used. Unlike the random look that characterizes "Hills and Valleys" mokume gane, stamping imparts distinct patterns. Using several colors creates the most interesting stamping effects, but for starters, this demo combines just three. You may want to substitute a different trio of colors; choose any that blend well together. And while I decorated an address book and pen, other types of book covers are equally good candidates for this process.

1 Prepare a Skinner Blend sheet of clay, approximately 2" × 6", on the thickest setting of your pasta machine.

2 Following the Skinner Blend instructions, fold and roll the sheet through the pasta machine to achieve a blended sheet.

3 Fold the sheet in half, matching like colors. Beginning with the dark end, roll the sheet through the machine at incrementally thinner settings until you have a paper-thin sheet. This will create a very long sheet, blending from one color through the others.

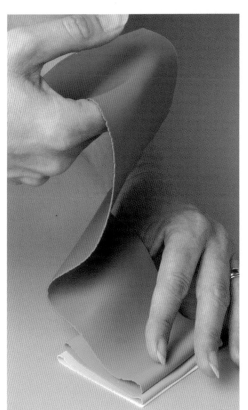

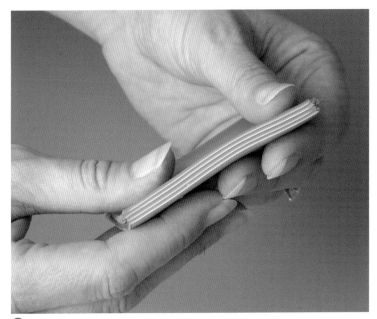

5 Cut the sheet formed in half and stack the clay, producing many layers of color.

4 Fold the sheet accordion style to create a blended block of clay, approximately 3" square. Turn the block to a side that has no folds, so as not to trap air in the clay. Roll this block through the pasta machine on the thickest setting to unite all the layers.

6 Mist the texture sheet and the back of the clay with water. Place the clay sheet down on the texture sheet and roll firmly with an acrylic rod. Pass over the clay only once to ensure that no double images occur.

7 Lift the clay sheet gently from the texturing sheet.

8 Carefully shave off the layers of clay with a very sharp blade to reveal a pattern that is appealing.

9 Roll the sheet through the pasta machine on a setting that is just slightly thinner than your finished shaved sheet. This will smooth the surface of the sheet without distorting the image. Save the shavings to adorn other items. Bake as per the clay manufacturer's instructions.

JUDY BELCHER

Completed Mokume Gane Texture Stamping: Of the numerous objects that might be adorned with a sheet of textured polymer clay, here, I've chosen an ordinary spiral-bound address book and ballpoint pen to transform into a pair of matching gifts. The book cover incorporates the demonstration sheet of clay and is accented by a border using the same process. The raw clay sheets were affixed to the book with a thin layer of white glue. The shavings were used to decorate the pen.

KEITH LAMBERTSON AND CAT GLAZER
Summer pin, made of 22k gold and diamonds as part of their "Faces of Nature" series, is a fine example of this husband-and-wife's award-winning cloisonné enamel jewelry. The luminous, multicolored depths of their creations provide inspiration for many polymer clay artists. PHOTO BY RALPH GABRINER

ENAMELING IS the art of using a glass "paste," or frit, and fusing it to a metal surface with heat. As with the formation of glass, enameling also has folklore attached to its origins. Some say it may have been invented accidentally, when sand and clay melted and fused to a piece of iron. Others believe that ancient Egyptian artisans just thought that glass or other jewels looked better with a shiny piece of metal placed behind them.

There are many enameling techniques, each with its own unique characteristics. Referred to by their French names, cloisonné ("partitioned") and plique-à-jour ("daylight openwork fold") are techniques that use metal to form a cell that is filled with enamel. In champlevé ("raised ground") and guilloche ("engine turning") or basse-taille ("low cut"), the metal is ground away and the remaining cavity is then filled with enamel.

CLOISONNÉ AND PLIQUE-À-JOUR

Developed in ancient Egypt, cloisonné is the oldest enameling method. It replicates the look of fine jewels by forming a pattern of compartments, or cells, separated by thin metal strips soldered to a metal base, then filled in with crushed glass in various colors.

Plique-à-jour is one of the most beautiful and difficult enameling techniques. It employs the same type of metal cells as cloisonné, but is not backed by metal. Therefore, with light showing through, the resulting piece of art mimics the beautiful effects of a stained-glass window—hence its French "daylight" name.

CHAMPLEVÉ AND GUILLOCHE, OR BASSE-TAILLE

Champlevé differs from cloisonné in that the desired pattern is gouged into a thick metal base, leaving a thin outline and channels that are then filled with enamel. This technique was highly prized during the Middle Ages as a traditional Celtic art form.

Guilloche, or basse-taille, is a more complex version of champlevé. The metal surface is cut away, and intricate circular patterns are then engraved in low relief. The enamel used is translucent and is filled until flush with the surrounding metal. The engraved pattern is enhanced by the tonal quality of its various levels of enamel, lending a feeling of great depth. Some of the best examples of this technique were created in the studios of the Russian jeweler Karl Fabergé.

Using Scrap Clay

Make good use of the piles of clay left over from previous projects by applying them to future work. Scraps of clay can be used to make another color less intense; to form the base on which a decorative layer of clay is added; or to make a mold, as I've done in the next demonstration. The most important thing to remember when conditioning scrap clay for a project is to remove *all* of the air pockets trapped in the clay. Start by cutting the scrap clay into manageable piles. To condition, fold a pile in half and run it through your pasta machine, turning it so the folded side is at a right angle to the rollers. Run the clay through your pasta machine many more times.

With an acrylic rod, smooth each pile of scrap clay to the approximate thickness of the thickest setting on your pasta machine.

Before each pass through the machine, stretch the clay to release any air that might be trapped under the surface.

SUPPLIES

conditioned scrap clay

water spritzer

acrylic roller

texturing sheet

sharp blade

shape cutters

platinum powder

paintbrush

protective mask

Kato Clear Polyclay Medium

tinting inks in purple, green, and blue

small mixing cups

pointed tool

Gloss Flecto Varathane clear finish

DEMONSTRATION Enamel Pin

I wanted to replicate the beauty of both cloisonné and basse-taille enamel in a polymer clay pin, being very drawn to the shimmering texture beneath the surface of the enamel. First I formed a cavity to hold the liquid polymer clay; then, to produce texture beneath the pool of liquid clay, I made my own mold out of scrap clay and textured its surface so the positive clay image would have texture in low relief. A texture sheet with small, deep images worked well; I used Clearsnap's "Waves and Weaves," which they call a molding mat, but other brands of texture sheets may be substituted. Where the clay is concerned, since this demo involves a pulverized metallic powder (I used Houston's) that may not adhere to all types of polymer clay, be sure to pretest the clay you choose. I have found that Kato Polyclay is the one that works well for me.

1 After spraying a texturing sheet with a fine mist of water and misting the back of the clay as well, impress the clay into the texturing sheet with an acrylic rod. Texturing sheets offer various patterns to choose from.

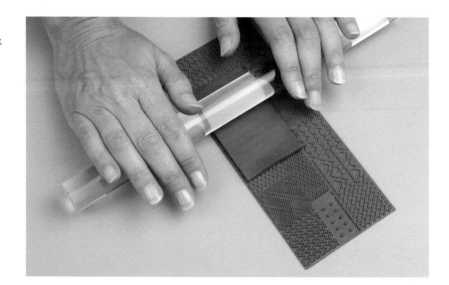

2 Cut apart the various blocks of texture into interesting shapes to form the mold. I drew out the shape of the jewelry item being created, a pin, and cut the pieces to match that pattern. Then I used shape cutters to make holes that would translate into raised areas of the finished work.

3 Position the various pieces on another sheet of scrap clay, leaving at least a $^1/_8$-inch gap between the elements. This will act as the "cloisonné wire" to form the pin's separate cells. Add an outer edge of scrap clay all the way around, leaving that same $^1/_8$-inch gap to form the outer border of the piece. Bake the mold for 30 minutes at 275 degrees; let it cool.

4 Mist the mold with water. Mist the back of a well-conditioned sheet of scrap clay, and lay it over the mold. Press the clay firmly into the mold with your fingers to ensure that every edge is properly formed. Cut away any excess clay around the edges. Allow water to dry.

5 With a dry paintbrush, dust the piece entirely with pulverized platinum powder. Metal powders become airborne easily, so be sure to wear a protective mask when working with this material. Follow the instructions provided by the manufacturer. Bake for 30 minutes at 275 degrees. Allow the piece to cool.

6 Prepare tinted liquid polymer clay: I used Ranger's alcohol inks, one small drop per ¹/₂-oz. of liquid clay. With a pointed tool, apply the tinted liquid drop-by-drop into the chosen cell. Wait for each series of drops to settle; add liquid until the cell is filled. Tap the bottom of the piece gently with your pointed tool to force the air bubbles to the surface; pop them with a fine pin prior to baking. As each cell is filled, bake between applications for 20 minutes at 275 degrees. Allow the piece to cool. Applying a coat of gloss finish seals the "metal" and adds the glass effect of the "enamel."

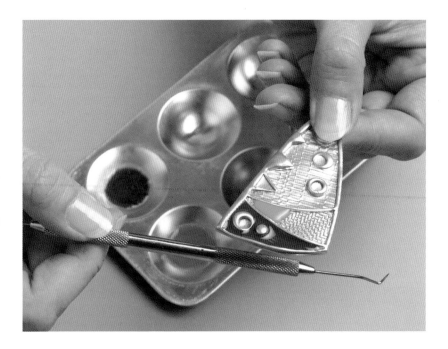

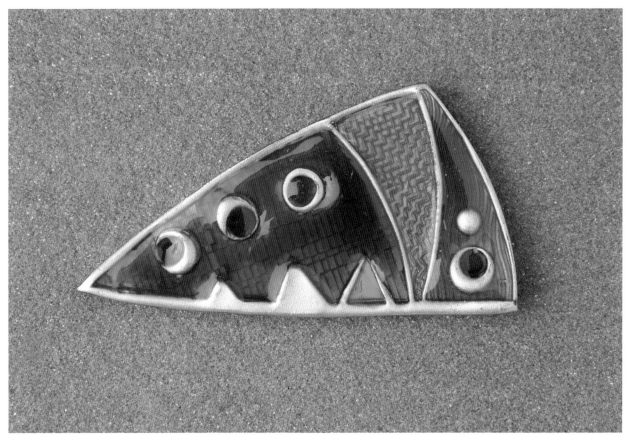

JUDY BELCHER
Completed Enamel Pin: Notice the shimmer of light catching the texture underneath the "enamel." That effect is enhanced by sealing polymer with gloss finish, as I did with this piece.

ANNEALING METAL POWDER

I USE PULVERIZED metal powders for various applications with polymer clay; they anneal to its surface when baked at temperatures slightly higher than those used for polymer clay, so test your brand of clay prior to trying this technique. Such pieces can also be given a patina wash with liquid antiquing solutions like Sophisticated Finishes. Metal powders may also be used to highlight only certain areas of the raw clay.

JUDY BELCHER
For this necklace, I imprinted a thin sheet of blended clay with the Clearsnap Molding Mat "Mandalas," using both heat-set black permanent ink and Pale Gold Metal Powders. I cut several 3" triangles from the sheet and "dragged" each of their edges through the metal powders. Then I rolled up the bead, beginning at the widest end and ending with the point of the triangle. Notice the metallic "shine" on the sides of the beads. This really makes the necklace shimmer and sparkle.

Metal Traditions in Polymer Clay

JUDY KUSKIN *Landscape Necklace* was inspired by nature's colors and textures around the artist's Seattle home. Her sophisticated jewelry is based on a marriage of hand-worked sterling silver and subtly textured polymer clay. PHOTO BY ROGER SCHREIBER

DEBORAH BRAMS *Gold Accents:* Adding touches of 22k goldleaf to a simple geometric pattern gives this polymer clay pin-and-earrings ensemble extra charm.

LISA PAVELKA

Heartfelt: Manipulating thin layers of polymer clay produced the flecks of white that peep through this pastel mokume gane pattern. The layers of clay were applied to a purchased small metal purse.

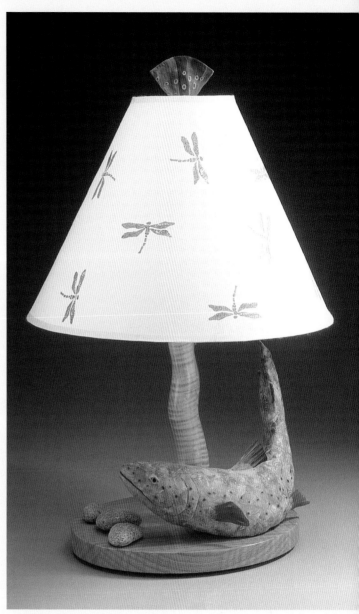

J. M. SYRON AND BONNIE BISHOFF

Brooktrout Lamp, by a husband-and-wife team who are best known for their furniture creations, incorporates the mokume gane technique with silver leaf to form the polymer clay scales on the fish at the base of the wooden lamp. PHOTO BY DEAN POWELL

SUE KELSEY

Metallic Mimic: Whimsically attaching a real metal zipper to a metallic-look vase turns a polymer clay piece into a Surrealist work of art.

3

FIBER
Traditions

Fiber is a general term that pertains here not only to cloth, but also to basketry and paper objects. Among the cloths that inspire polymer clay artists are the distinctive ikat fabrics that have origins in Malaysia and beautiful batiks from Indonesia. Another source of inspiration are traditional fabrics from Africa, such as colorful kente cloth and bold mudcloth patterns.

Many other styles of surface designs applied to fabric with dyes and inks also provide great ideas for clay artists. The theme of the pattern can be reflected in millefiori cane slices or combined to replicate a whole piece of cloth. Such designs created in clay can be as basic as a checkerboard cane that suggests gingham or plaid or as complex as a landscape scene translated into canework. Other styles of woven and dyed fabrics will be covered in the detailed demonstrations that lie ahead.

Baskets made of straw or other fibers offer equally exciting patterns for the clay artist to replicate, as do certain printed textiles that resemble woven basketry. Copying the way strands of such fibers weave in and out in intricate, interlacing patterns is especially challenging when integrating multiple colors of clay.

Paper items also inspire clay artists. The word paper derives from the Latin *papyrus,* a plant that was sliced and pressed into sheets used by the Egyptians as the first known surface on which writing could be applied. Paper, as we know it today, was developed many centuries later in China.

SUSAN HYDE
Textile designs inspired the patterns on this polymer clay figure. PHOTO BY ROGER SCHREIBER

IKAT, a Malay word meaning to tie or bind, describes the time-consuming process whereby bundled threads are tie-dyed in various colors that are then woven into a distinctive, diffused pattern. Many polymer clay artists replicate ikat with canework. The look can be accomplished in many ways, but the goal is to have a subtle repeat pattern that appears to be woven. One way to make a cane that can be recombined into many ikat patterns is to prepare sheets of clay as though making a Skinner Blend. But rather than blending the entire sheet, roll it through the pasta machine only five or six times.

Here, equal parts of violet and white are the basis for an ikat pattern. The same effect can be completed with other color combinations.

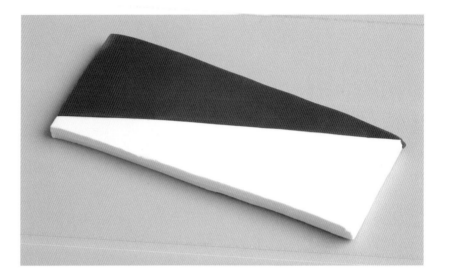

The resulting sheet will have a woven effect that can then be cut and stacked so that every other sheet is slightly offset to form an ikat cane. Trim the excess clay to form a rectangular slab and reduce and recombine into many interesting patterns.

LEFT *Authentic Ikat:* An example of traditional Indonesian ikat textile design provided by Cynthia Toops is reflected in her artistry inspired by it *(below)*. PHOTO BY DAN ADAMS

BELOW CYNTHIA TOOPS

Interpreted Ikat: The artist created her fine interpretation of a classic ikat pattern by designing it on polymer clay, then slicing it into numerous slivers and recombining them to form this imaginative bracelet. PHOTO BY DAN ADAMS

BARGELLO

WHEN CLOTH INSPIRES polymer clay artists, one favorite category is the stitched pattern called *bargello,* a decorative zigzag design that is woven into, or stitched onto, fabric. Named for the Palazzo Bargello in Florence, the flamelike design appears on handsome seventeenth-century upholstered chairs housed there.

When needlepoint experts employ the bargello stitch, the visual effects can be dazzling, as wool strands of numerous color gradations zigzag into striking patterns. Equally beautiful are the imaginative polymer clay interpretations of bargello shown in the colorful examples below.

LAURA LISKA
Sheets of blended polymer clay were cut and combined to replicate the look of bargello in these variously shaped beads.

KIM CAVENDER
Shaded strips of polymer clay were used to construct bargello canes for this bracelet, joined with silver and glass beads.

TRADITIONAL AFRICAN tribal fabrics have inspired many artists with their rich designs steeped in ceremonial meanings. Kente cloth, made in Ghana, is one such fabric. The word comes from *kenten,* which means basket, aptly named to suggest the cloth's resemblance to woven basketry patterns. Kente designs often signify the gender and social status of the wearer, and sometimes reflect historical events.

A basket-weave design can be replicated in polymer clay canework using a blended square and recombining it into a basket-weave pattern. Prepare a Skinner Blend bull's-eye cane, then slice off opposite sides of the cylinder to form a square. When the cane is flattened with an acrylic rod into a square, it has two opposing darker sides and two lighter sides. The cane is then reduced and cut into four equal sections, as shown below.

Authentic Kente Cloth, as shown in this fine example, has a distinctive pattern that resembles woven basketry. Variations may include narrative designs depicting traditional African tribal events.

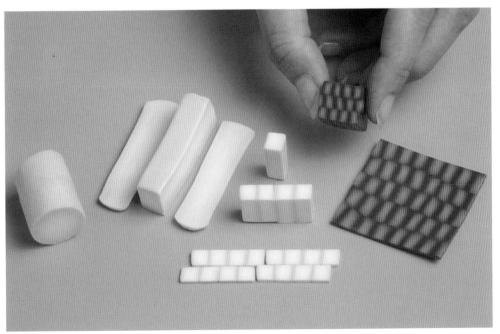

Stack the sections side by side, making sure the darker sides of the cane touch, and roll gently with an acrylic rod to adhere the sides. By taking thin slices of the cane and lining them up to form a basket-weave pattern, a whole sheet can be formed and used to embellish any project.

ANOTHER AFRICAN tribal fabric is known as mudcloth, originated by the women of Mali. *Bogolanfini* is its native name, which translates to "cotton cloth dyed with mud," a centuries-old process based on numerous applications of plant juices and mud to pattern handwoven cotton cloth. Many patterns come from storytelling themes, each with its own meaning and colors, although the most traditional mudcloth palette is black and white.

SUPPLIES

black polymer clay

white polymer clay

black/white mixture formed into gray clay

pasta machine

acrylic rod

texture sheet with geometric patterns

water spritzer

sharp blade

wood picture frame

white glue

DEMONSTRATION

Black-and-White Mudcloth

I love the geometric patterns of mudcloth and enjoy combining several into one art piece—in this case, a picture frame—that tells my own story in polymer clay.

1 Roll out a sheet of white clay on the largest setting of your pasta machine. Roll out a sheet each of gray and black clay on a very thin setting. The sheets should be about the size of your texture sheet.

2 To adhere the gray and black sheets together, roll them through the machine again on a very thin setting.

3 With an acrylic rod, adhere the black and gray sheet, black side up, to the white sheet of clay. Choose a texture sheet with bold geometric patterns. Clearsnap has a large variety that are perfectly suited to this project.

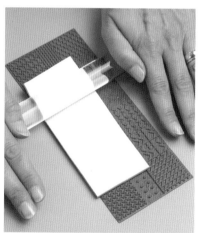

4 After spraying the texture sheet with a fine mist of water, lay the black side of the clay against it and also spray that with a fine mist of water. Then roll the clay firmly with an acrylic rod to impress the texture sheet's pattern deep into the clay.

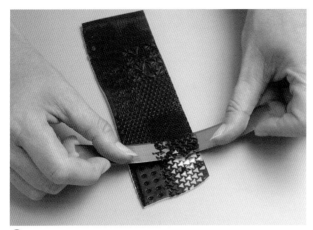

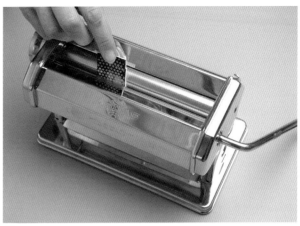

5 With a sharp blade, carefully shave off just the raised areas of clay. Work in small sections, or cut the sheet apart and work on them separately. Don't cut too deeply, as some of the black must remain to form the pattern. Impressing texture into the black surface and carefully shaving off its raised areas will reveal the white clay and a design similar to that of mudcloth.

6 Roll the finished sheet through the pasta machine, beginning with the thickest setting and resetting it to incrementally thinner settings until the sheet is smooth.

JUDY BELCHER
Completed Mudcloth: For my frame, I cut my finished sheet into rectangles of irregular sizes and applied them to the prepared wood frame, then baked it for 30 minutes at 275 degrees. To prepare the wood frame (or any wood object on which clay affixes), bake the wood for 20 minutes at 275 degrees to ensure its dryness, and check for warping. Then apply a thin layer of white glue and allow to dry. (That smiling blonde is Georgia, the daughter of my photographer, Steve Payne.)

LEFT *Authentic Mudcloth,* such as this example, is actually dyed with a mixture of plant juices and mud. The patterns often reflect African story-telling themes handed down through the ages.

Mudcloth Beads

SUPPLIES

polymer clays:
translucent, white,
yellow, brown

thin knitting needle

Kato Repel Gel

fine paintbrush

protective gloves

brown and black inks

cotton pad

old toothbrush

While researching the history of traditional mudcloth, I found many references to trade beads made from bone and dyed in the traditional fiber method. The beads generally bear the same patterns as the fabrics, but on a much smaller scale, as you'll see in this demo. I chose to use a resist method involving a clear resist gel, and applied brown and black inks to polymer clay to simulate bone mudcloth beads.

❶ Blend white clay with a pinch of yellow and brown to form an ivory-colored blend. Mix in an equal part of translucent clay and knead to give it a grainy effect. Shape the clay into some beads. Of the two shown, the bonelike bead will be decorated here. Pierce that bead with the knitting needle to make the hole. Leave the bead on the needle for baking; it will be easier to handle for the resist and dyeing process. Bake for 30 minutes at 275 degrees. Allow it to cool.

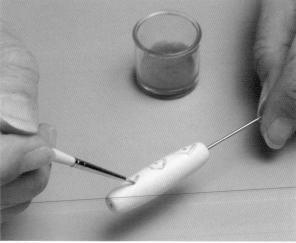

❷ With a fine point on your brush, paint a design on the bead with Repel Gel, which acts as a resist. (Because the gel is clear, I have tinted it with blue powder so the design will show for the camera. This is not necessary, but will clarify where the design has been applied. It does not affect the final result.)

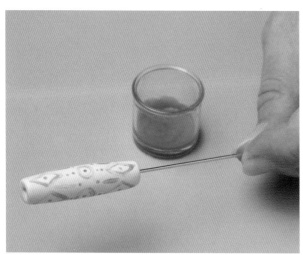

❸ After completing your design, allow the gel to dry. It takes about fifteen minutes.

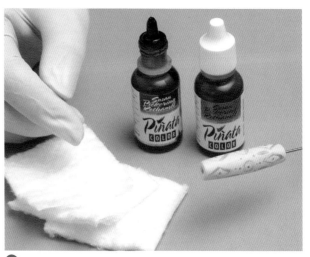

❹ Put on protective gloves, and have a few cotton pads ready for applying the inks. These Piñata inks are Burro Brown and Mantilla Black.

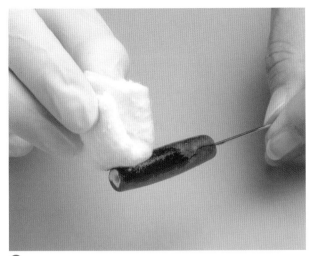

5 With a cotton pad and a dabbing motion, apply a coat of brown ink. Dab gently so as not to disturb the Repel Gel. Using the same dabbing motion, apply a coat of black ink immediately. Alcohol inks dry almost on contact. The brown base color gives a more subtle "mud" effect.

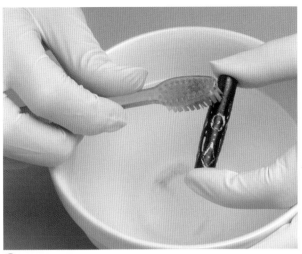

6 Rinse and scrub the bead with a toothbrush and water to remove the Repel Gel and reveal the image.

JUDY BELCHER
Completed Mudbead on Keyring: When you create other beads based on this technique, you may want to experiment with varying their colors and assembling in one well-coordinated bracelet or necklace.

I HAVE ALWAYS BEEN intrigued by the unique patterns of batik fabrics. Most closely associated with the Indonesian island of Java, batik fabrics are pattern-dyed by means of a hot-wax-resist process. By boiling off the wax, the design stands out in the original color of the fabric, and the process may be repeated to include several colors.

For my first experiment with polymer clay to imitate batik, I used clear liquid clay to act as the resist on white fabric. Since the fabric must be hot before starting the project, I heated it up in my oven at 275 degrees for 15 minutes. (I always test fabric this way, to make sure that heat doesn't shrink or melt it.) Heat also causes the liquid clay to set up more quickly and keep the drawn lines from bleeding. After cutting enough fabric for the project I had in mind, a beach bag, I drew my initial design on it with liquid clay, then returned the fabric to my oven for ten minutes to set the design. When it cooled, I applied Kato Clear Liquid Medium tinted with alcohol inks to "dye" the rest of the fabric. An advantage of polymer clay in liquid form is that it won't chip off or make the fabric rigid.

TIP

Use latex gloves to spread liquid clay and blend lines where two colors meet. Using gloves also conserves the liquid clay, as none is absorbed into an applicator.

JUDY BELCHER
Beach Bag. The process described above produced this batik-inspired bag. After taking a length of white cotton fabric through all the necessary steps, I cut, pieced, and stitched it, sewing on the handles last. Using liquid polymer clay offers the added benefit of making the fabric water-proof—hence, a good material for a beach bag holding a wet towel, as shown here.

Batik Jewelry

SUPPLIES
white polymer clay
glass tile
thin knitting needle
Kato Repel Gel
fine paintbrush
yellow and magenta inks
cotton pad
old toothbrush

My second experiment with batik was similar to that of the mudcloth beads. I used repel gel to act as a resist when applying alcohol inks to a base bead of unbaked white clay. In this case, the base bead was round, and the process comprises three easy steps. (Notice that the mudcloth beads were baked first, and then the resist and inks are applied, whereas with the batik beads, the resist and inks are applied prior to baking. Other than the possible distortion of the bead if it is not baked first, the result is the same.)

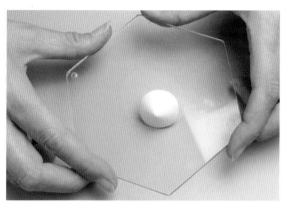

1 To form white clay into beads, place a tile of clear glass (or Plexiglas) over a rounded ball of clay and move it in a circular motion while applying slight pressure. This makes a lovely bicone bead—that is, a bead with a point on each end.

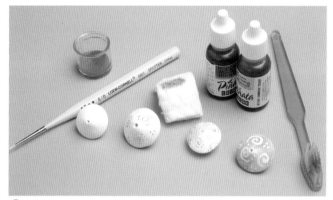

2 Puncture threading holes in the beads with a thin knitting needle. Use Kato Repel Gel and a fine paintbrush to design the beads. (I tinted the clear gel with blue powder so the design would show for the camera.) After the gel dries, apply colored inks (these are Piñata Sunbright Yellow and Señorita Magenta) and blend them with a cotton pad. Bake the beads for 30 minutes at 275 degrees. When the beads are cool, rinse them and scrub off the repel gel with a toothbrush.

JUDY BELCHER
Completed Batik Jewelry: A warm, subtle palette helps give the look of batik to these polymer clay pieces. The earrings are finished with silver wires; the beads are being strung with strands of fine yellow cord.

FASTENING TWO PIECES of fabric together with some type of stuffing in between goes back to ancient times. The technique was used mostly to add warmth to clothing in Northern China or, in Europe, to give extra safety padding to a doublet worn under armor. Although its roots lie abroad, quilting became a truly American craft when Colonial women began fashioning a top layer of cloth pieced into geometric patterns attached to a solid bottom sheet of cloth, with stuffing, or batting, sandwiched between. The region in which I live is steeped in this rich needlework heritage. There are more than three hundred West Virginia artisans preserving the tradition as they painstakingly employ time-honored stitching methods to create goods for the Cabin Creek Quilters Cooperative. With such brilliant examples so near at hand, quilting became a natural source of ideas for my earliest polymer clay work.

Long after I began polymer clay projects based on traditional quilt blocks, I was led farther down the quilting path when I found that it's possible to machine-stitch sheets of polymer clay. I have my daughter to thank for that discovery. Maria was working on a science-fair project about the flexural strength of polymer clays, so she experimented by baking very thin sheets of different brands. When she commented that Kato clay felt like leather when removed from the oven, a lightbulb went on in my head: Maybe clay could be sewn like leather? I ran to my sewing machine immediately and tried it. It worked! Since I enjoy sewing, but am an impatient person, I had always found the quilting process too exacting, matching up all the pieces by cutting them precisely. Here was the perfect solution. When I quilt with polymer, the raw pieces of clay are forgiving and adjustable. If a corner doesn't fit just right, I give it a nudge and the pieces will meet. Try it for yourself and see.

MARCIA WALL
My cousin Marcia is an expert quilter. She usually chooses watercolor fabrics for her stunning wall hangings such as this one—a wonderful source of inspiration for my polymer clay adaptations.

JUDY BELCHER
This quilt block and ornament made of polymer clay canes are pieces I was asked to contribute to decorate the West Virginia tree at the White House several years ago.

JUDY BELCHER
Purses: This collection of quilt-inspired, machine-stitched polymer clay purses includes (upper right) the duffle bag for which the demonstration quilt block (on pages 68–69) was created.

SUPPLIES

polymer clays: white, green, turquoise, violet

pasta machine

basic quilt pattern

heavy-weight template paper

white work paper, two sheets

sharp blade

violet backing fabric

fleece batting

sewing machine

thread

scissors

clear liquid clay

DEMONSTRATION # Stitched Clay Quilting

This is a simple way to practice quilting with clay and still have the design flexibility that fabric allows. I like to use Skinner Blend sheets of clay for my quilt patterns to simulate a watercolor look. For this demo, I chose three colors, plus white, for my polymer quilting blocks, then stitched them onto fabric and turned it into a duffle bag for my daughter. Instead of the basic geometric patterns shown, if you want to see others, a good source is quilter Alex Anderson's Website. You may also decide to substitute colors of your own choice and stitch your polymer quilting onto coordinated fabric for a vest, handbag, or other fashionable items.

TIP

For this project, you must have a sewing machine that can sew through denim-weight fabric. Practice on a scrap piece of baked clay to adjust your tension and stitch length. Once you sew the clay, you cannot go back and remove the stitches and try again, as you can with fabric. And as suggested earlier, remember to oven-test the backing fabric you plan to use.

1 Prepare three Skinner Blend sheets. To achieve a watercolor gradation, stop running the clay sheets through your pasta machine while the blend is still streaky. That will provide a range of tones in each color.

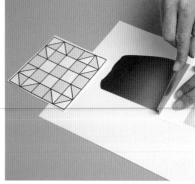

2 Design a template on heavy-weight paper, ruling each little block 1 1/2" square. With your blended clay placed on white work paper, begin to cut squares in dark, light, and medium tones of each color, using the template as your guide.

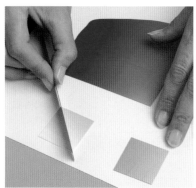

3 Consult the pattern to determine how many squares are to be cut diagonally.

4 Carefully transfer the squares to a clean sheet of paper. Position them so they fit as closely together as possible. If any of the seams do not meet, rub their edges slightly to smooth them together at the join. Bake the seamless square for 25 minutes at 275 degrees, and let it cool.

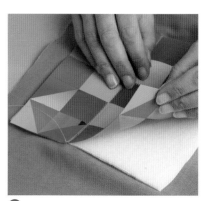

5 This optional step will give your quilt depth. With your backing fabric in place, put a square of fleece down, then lay the quilt block on top of it.

6 Set the tension on your machine at a low setting; the stitch length at $1/16$"; and the zigzag feature at $1/8$". Sew the clay to the fabric (with fleece between), clay side up. Follow the quilt pattern, keeping the center mark on the machine foot in line with the "seams" of the quilt pattern. Sew across the middle of the clay first, then give the pattern a quarter turn and sew across the middle, crossing the stitches made in the first pass to join the clay evenly to the fabric. Tie the threads by pulling the top one through to the back and securing it with a double knot.

7 Finally, sew around the entire quilt block to fasten it securely to the fabric. If the foot of your sewing machine left faint scratches on the clay, rub the surface with a small amount of liquid clay and buff off the excess with a paper towel. Return the piece to the oven for 5 minutes to "erase" any scratches and give the piece a more supple, leatherlike look.

JUDY BELCHER
These are just a few variations among the numerous basic quilting patterns that may be transferred easily into polymer clay blocks and sewn on fabric.

Fiber Traditions in Polymer Clay

RIGHT **ROBERT WILEY**

Christmas Trees: Rubber stamps made by SAR (Some Assembly Required), a company whose products are used with paper, inspired these beautiful earrings. The artist explains, "I've been able to develop a technique for using these stamps with polymer clay"—a method he employs with obvious success. PHOTO BY RICK WELLS

BELOW **DEBBIE JACKSON**

Faux Fibers: Resembling fine decorative papers and favorite fabric swatches, this unique necklace made of polymer clay shows both the artist's expertise with her craft and her innovative way of combining clay with interesting fibers. PHOTO BY DIANE LUFTIG

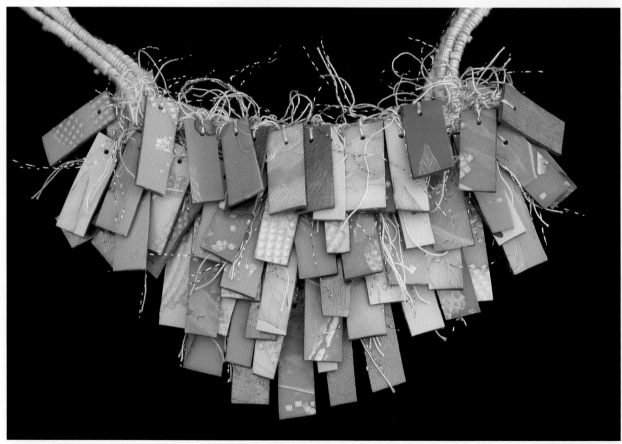

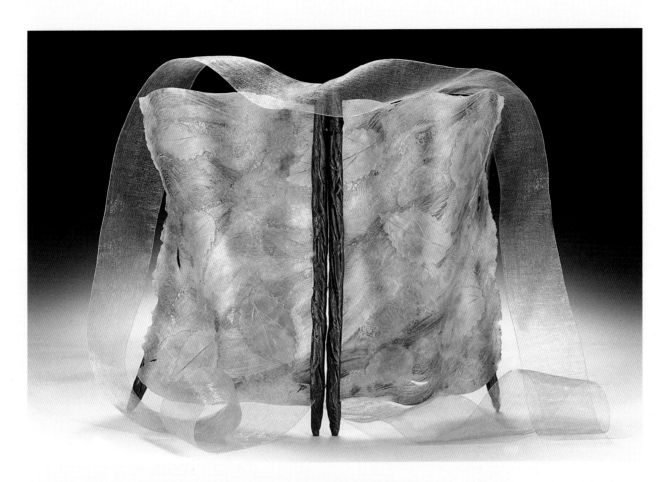

ABOVE **ELISE WINTERS**
Mini Screen: Thin, translucent sheets that resemble handmade paper, and like their inspiration, also incorporate other materials, evolved into this delicate, shoji-like miniature screen of polymer clay. PHOTO BY RALPH GABRINER

LEFT **MARCIA LASKA**
Vellum Paper inspired this stylish, functional bowl made with layers of translucent clay. PHOTO BY RICK LEE

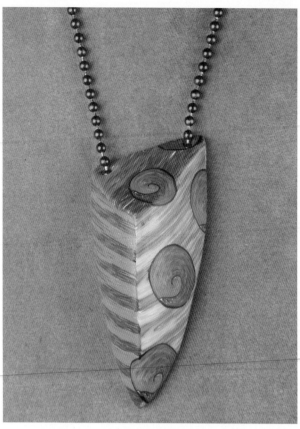

DONNA KATO

Faux Ikat: Bright colors and the artist's skilled technique give this polymer clay pendant its dramatic pattern, based on ikat fabrics.

SUSAN HYDE

Dancing Woman: Textile designs from various sources are interpreted in the skilled application of intricate artwork in this appealing polymer clay figure, further embellished with clay jewelry. PHOTO BY ROGER SCHREIBER

NANCY OSBAHR

Quilt-Inspired Heart Pins: These multi-patterned creations are based on colorful quilts. PHOTO BY JOE COCA

CAROL SIMMONS
Fanciful Scenes: "I love landscape quilts, but find sewing tedious," this artist says. "So, now, I make my 'fabrics' out of polymer clay." She takes thin slices, cuts them to shape, and combines them to create these fanciful scenes, using millefiori techniques.

JUDY BELCHER
Block Bracelet: Similar quilt patterns rendered in different colors add visual appeal to this polymer clay bracelet. Black-and-white borders unify the blocks, which are held together with glass beads.

STEVEN FORD AND DAVID FORLANO
Beach Balls, 14×9×6" in diameter, are made of polymer clay. The forms were assembled with the aid of an ordinary sewing machine, using a zigzag stitch.
PHOTO BY ARTISTS

MAGS BONHAM
Spirit Box is based on quilt-inspired canes. The artist inflated the unique little box with a puff of air prior to baking, then cut the lid after baking.

CYNTHIA BECKER
Picture Pendant: This paper photo transfer on polymer clay shows Chief Ouray of the Ute tribe and his wife, Chipeta, as photographed in 1880 by the Mathew Brady studio. The pendant is a clever mirror image of the pose on the right side of the glass negative.

ABOVE SUSAN HYDE
These swatches from the artist's polymer canes feature her colorful flamework patterns.

LEFT PATRICIA ECHEAGARAY
Woven Basket simulates basketry's intricate, interlacing patterns in polymer clay. PHOTO BY ARTIST

4

PAINTING AND DRAWING
Traditions

If you find yourself in need of inspiration for your next polymer clay project, go to a museum and look at paintings. If you don't live near a museum, wonderful art is as close as a click away on your computer or may be found in books at your local library. Study the works of the masters viewed up close and from a distance. In each painting or drawing you might find ideas in the subject matter, composition, design, or color choices. In translating artwork into clay projects, in addition to making wall hangings that simulate paintings or drawings, create jewelry, purses, and other objects based on a particular artist's work or the style of an art movement.

Do you favor paintings of people, nature, or inanimate objects in still-life art? Do you prefer realistic, abstract, or completely nonobjective pictures? Perhaps technique will stimulate your imagination: paint that is textured, layered, applied flat, or just the opposite—filled with contours and perspective. The medium itself may trigger ideas. Did the artist use watercolors, acrylics, oils, pastels, pen and ink, graphite, or mixed media?

Finally, adapting the overall essence of a great artist's work may be the thing that gets you started, as it did in my case. I chose to make five polymer clay purses that pay homage to five famous artists. Each artist has a distinct style that differs from all others. As illustrated in the five projects that lie ahead, they all offer a wealth of ideas to stimulate your own creations.

BARBARA A. MCGUIRE
Powerful Portrait is a polymer clay inset panel of a hand-made book banded in silk ribbon. PHOTO BY ARTIST

GEORGIA O'KEEFFE

ALTHOUGH SHE PAINTED numerous landscapes depicting her beloved Southwest, Georgia O'Keeffe is best known for her sensuous paintings of abstracted, oversized flowers, which usually fill every inch of her canvas, leaving just a little background at the edges. I am particularly drawn to her manipulation of line, color, and the subtle shadings on her floral canvases, which look as much like delicate watercolors as they do the rich oil paintings that they are.

DEMONSTRATION O'Keeffe Flowers

SUPPLIES

polymer clays: blue, green, pearl

pasta machine

sharp blade

purse to adorn

two-part epoxy

To replicate the essence of O'Keeffe flowers in polymer clay, I used a Skinner Blend bull's-eye cane for their petals, being careful to have the blend tint only the outer edges of the cane slightly. The center of each petal is the same pearl white as the base of the purse to give the flowers a painterly effect of blending into the background. The purse that I adorned is made of chipboard, covered in satin. I removed the satin and worked directly on the chipboard, but polymer clay flowers, or any clay embellishment, may be glued directly to fabric.

1 Mix blue with pearl white to produce a subtle hue. Create a Skinner Blend (see page 19) by curving the blade for an arc of color when blended. After the clay is well blended, give the sheet a one-quarter turn so the pearl edge leads into the pasta machine, and roll at incrementally thinner settings until a very thin sheet is formed.

2 Roll a core cylinder of pearl clay about an inch in circumference and wrap with the blended sheet, beginning with the pearl end. This should result in a thin tinting of the outer edge of the bull's-eye cane. Kato clay can be rolled and baked in very thin sheets and still maintain its form and flexibility.

3 Allow the cane to rest briefly. Slice thinly to form each petal. Roll each slice through the pasta machine at incrementally thinner settings, until very delicate petals are formed. Stretch some to vary their shapes and sizes, producing a more interesting and varied array of petals.

4 Pinch the end of each petal to give it depth, and place them around a center point to form the flower. Bake the flower for 20 minutes at 275 degrees.

JUDY BELCHER
Completed O'Keeffe Flowers: The pearl polymer clay background on the purse is an optional step. It's a layer of pattern, rubber-stamped on the clay and glued with two-step epoxy to the chipboard base. The flowers were glued on last.

GUSTAV KLIMT

GUSTAV KLIMT played a leading role in the Viennese Art Nouveau movement, also known as the Vienna Secession, a group of painters and artisans who rebelled against the conservative work of earlier generations. Klimt's work shows his love of intricate fabric patterns and the female form. His paintings exude rich gilding, bold colors, and highly decorative designs on clothing and backgrounds. He often drew the figures in his paintings as nudes in seductive poses, then painted clothing on them.

GUSTAV KLIMT (1862–1918)
The Kiss, 1907–1908, oil on canvas, 180 × 180 cm. Oesterreichische Galerie, Vienna, Austria. PHOTO BY ERICH LESSING / ART RESOURCE, NY

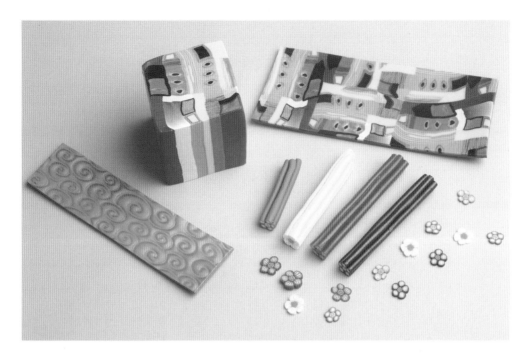

These polymer clay materials were combined to capture the Klimt spirit: a freely rendered geometric pattern dominated by yellows, oranges, and browns; wildly contrasting, brightly colored flower canes; and a clay sheet rubber-stamped to produce an undulating textural effect.

JUDY BELCHER
Mounted on a chipboard base, my Klimt-inspired polymer clay purse echoes the artist's most famous painting, *The Kiss,* and is further embellished with gold silk cord and clay beads at the closure.

DUTCH GRAPHIC ARTIST Maurits Cornelis Escher was world-famous for his drawings of visual puzzles that play with positive and negative shapes formed into intricate geometric patterns. One famous work shows a flock of birds flying over a landscape, but as the viewer's fascinated eye moves across the picture, the shapes of the birds suddenly transform themselves from figures in the sky into fields on the ground.

The repetitive nature of such designs would be easy to duplicate in canework if it were not for the way Escher manipulates his shapes in such complex ways. Canes are difficult to reduce and recombine when the sides are not equal, flat, or cylindrical. So I chose to use a simple repeating triangle with sides of equal length to form my cane for a multicolored Escher-like purse.

DEMONSTRATION Escher Geometric

SUPPLIES

polymer clays: green, yellow, violet, white, black, orange

circle, square, and triangle cutters

pasta machine

sharp blade

onionskin paper

purse to adorn

Since my Escher project begins in the same way as this chapter's first demo (see page 78), the two preliminary steps are not depicted again. To summarize those steps: Form Skinner Blend sheets (see page 19) for each of the colors used. When the clay is well blended, give each sheet a one-quarter turn so the white edge leads into the pasta machine and rolls at incrementally thinner settings, until very thin sheets are formed. Beginning with the white edge, roll the sheet up to form a Skinner Blend bull's-eye cane of each color.

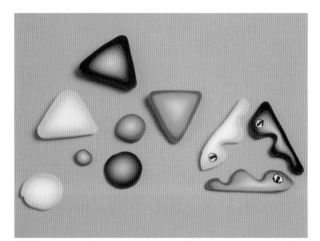

1 Cut each of the colored canes into two or more sections. Left, pinch the canes into triangles. Reduce by rolling the rest into various sizes. Right, work each cane into a squiggly form, leaving one flat side. An eye may be added using a small circle cutter to remove clay from the squiggly form; replace it with a small snake of black clay wrapped in white.

2 Embellish each cane, using various cutters to remove sections of the clay and replace with smaller blended bull's-eye canes. Form the individual canes into a triangle, with the flat side facing out. Fill in the empty spaces with white clay by rolling ropes of white clay in various thicknesses the same length as your cane. Insert them into the cane until it can be compressed into an equilateral triangle. Above are slices from the longer cane shown reduced on the following page.

3 Reduce the cane by compressing one side of it against the table and pinching and stretching the top, making sure to keep the triangle shape. Turn the cane to a different side and repeat the process until it is the desired size for your project.

4 Cut thin slices of the cane into six equal parts to form a hexagon; mirror each side when recombining. To make the slices adhere firmly to each other and to the base clay, rub their surfaces with onionskin paper (the kind bakeries use), which will also remove fingerprints. The cane recombined as a new cane on the right.

JUDY BELCHER
Completed Escher Geometric: After combining enough clay canes into a sheet sized to cover the front of a purse stripped to the chipboard, I bordered the panel with a pattern of stripes. Striped sheets of clay finished off the sides, back, and bottom. The entire purse was then baked for an hour at 275 degrees. The flexibility of polymer clay even allows it to be wrapped around the purse handles.

GEORGES SEURAT

GEORGES SEURAT was a classically trained painter, but instead of mixing colors on his palette, he applied his paint in a series of dots of pure color. When viewed at a distance, they seem to merge, creating a haze of brilliant color—a technique that became known as Pointillism.

In effect, Seurat approached painting not only as an art, but as a science, working out his canvases with exquisite precision, like mathematical exercises. When you see his work in a museum, as opposed to looking at it reproduced on the printed page of a book, if you examine a section of his canvas close up, it looks like a mass of dots that have no cohesion or meaning. But then, when you back away and view it at a distance, that shimmering jumble of colorful dots comes into focus as distinctive subject matter—people, places, and things that resonate with life. And what a challenge it is to simulate that remarkable technique in polymer clay.

GEORGES SEURAT (1859–1891)
A Sunday on La Grande Jatte, 1884–86, oil on canvas, 81³/₄" × 121" (207.5 × 308.1 cm). The Art Institute of Chicago.

DEMONSTRATION Seurat Pointillism

Duplicating this method in clay demands patience. Thirty-six hours into the piece demonstrated here, I was ready to give up, but with perseverance, I was rewarded with a "painting" of my daughter and me at a lake near our home. I added the umbrella to more closely suggest the famous Seurat painting shown opposite.

SUPPLIES

polymer clays: blue, green, red, white, black

acrylic roller

clay gun

sharp blade

scissors

needle tool

tweezers

purse

1 Make several Skinner Blends (see page 19), using various combinations of the colors. Roll the blends to form small cylinders of clay so one color is on top and gradually ends in the other color. Place a clay cylinder in a clay gun, using the smallest-diameter round disk to form long, spaghettilike strands of clay. Dust them with cornstarch and bake for 25 minutes at 275 degrees.

2 Cut each strand into ¹/₄" sections and keep each color family separate.

TIP

A good thickness for the white base clay is ¹/₃"; roll two sheets together to achieve that thickness. Sketch the picture lightly on the base with a needle tool, then embed each strand with a tweezer. Bake the finished piece for 30 minutes at 275 degrees.

JUDY BELCHER

Completed Seurat Pointillism: The finished polymer clay "painting" is embedded into a rectangular purse form, which I covered entirely with black clay. Then I pressed the image into the raw clay and baked the entire piece for 30 minutes at 275 degrees.

JACKSON POLLOCK

A POWERFUL FORCE in the Abstract Expressionist movement, Jackson Pollock sometimes mixed sand, broken glass, and other materials into his paint to create thick impasto textures. He taped his canvas to the floor and moved all around it like a dancer. His arms were always in motion as he flung and dripped mazes of paint onto his canvas. "Action Painting," the name given to Pollock's style, is said to reveal to the viewer the unconscious moods of the artist. "Drip" painting is the most familiar and descriptive term associated with his revolutionary work.

I first saw a Pollock painting during a museum visit when I was a teen, and I wondered why his work was considered art. But when I looked closer, I was drawn to the layers upon layers of paint that he used to achieve depths of pattern. There was no central focus to the huge canvas, so I spent a great deal of time moving along its length, scrutinizing its different sections. Little did I know then that, many years later, I would turn again to this dynamic work to make it the basis of a work of mine in polymer clay.

Creating my Pollock purse was fun. I wanted to achieve the overall look of his drip painting, so I chose to work on a large ceramic tile that could be trimmed and attached to a purse with liquid clay. I mixed liquid polymer clay with gold, silver, and pearl powdered pigments and black alcohol ink, then transferred the liquid into applicator bottles with dropper tips.

On a preheated ceramic tile, I drizzled and dripped one layer of each of the liquids, keeping my movements very fluid, then baked the tile for an additional five minutes and repeated the layering and baking process with each of the liquids, until I was pleased with the end result. Then I peeled the finished clay sheet from the ceramic tile and trimmed and adhered it to the purse with a thin layer of liquid clay, and baked the entire purse for 20 minutes at 275 degrees. I used pins to hold the clay sheet in place while baking.

JUDY BELCHER
Completed Pollock Action Painting: This purse was adorned with the pattern whose colors were created by mixing powdered pigments and black alcohol ink with liquid clay.

Painting and Drawing Traditions in Polymer Clay

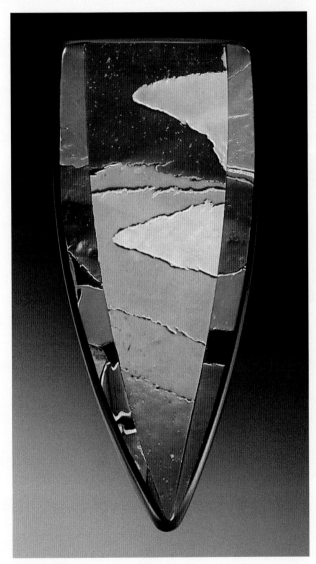

MAGGIE MAGGIO
Colorwash Pin (left) combines both watercolor and collage techniques in one compelling polymer clay piece. *Folk Art Beads* (right) have earthy tones inspired by watercolor painting. PHOTOS BY BILL BACHUBER

DIANE VILLANO
Miguel, made of
Premo! over papier
mâché, has clean, crisp
lines and bright primary
colors reminiscent
of Piet Mondrian's
abstract paintings.
PHOTO BY HAROLD SHAPIRO

DENISE GRAHAM
Blossoms as bold as
Van Gogh sunflowers
are interpreted in this
polymer clay painting
enclosed in a coordi-
nated self-frame.

SUZANNE IVESTER
Cliffs at Acapulco, 12"-x-16", is a hanging made of polymer clay on Masonite. PHOTO BY ARTIST

DONNA KATO
Painterly Pin: Component caning, a simplified form of layering, is featured in a polymer clay pin that has a bold, painterly style.

NANCY OSBAHR
Garden Series: As tribute to Donna Kato's work, above, this polymer clay tube necklace interprets its stylized floral design. PHOTO BY JOE COCA

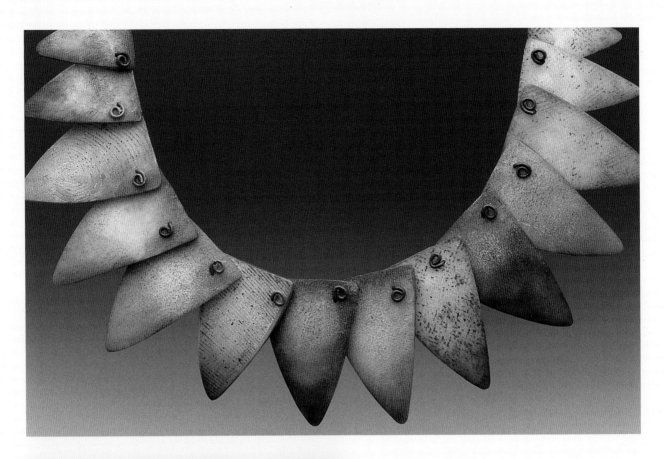

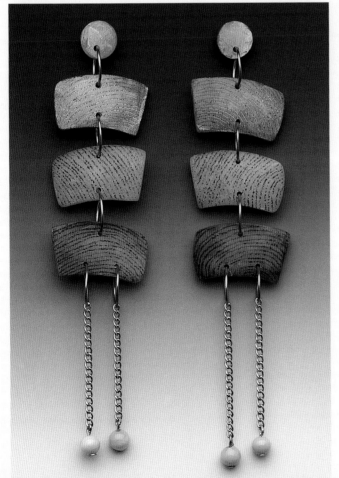

LOUISE FISCHER COZZI

Brushstrokes: The subtle colorations of an oil painting are emulated in these handsome polymer clay jewelry pieces.

PHOTOS BY GEORGE POST

KATHLEEN DUSTIN
Blue (opposite top) and *Molly* (opposite bottom) shoulder purses evoke, in polymer clay, the beauty of classic Renaissance portraiture—repeated (left) in miniature on this lovely neckpiece.
PHOTOS BY GEORGE POST

ABOVE MICHELLE ROSS
Wall Hanging: Alcohol inks contribute to the delicacy of this unique, watercolor-inspired polymer clay wall piece.

RIGHT MIKE BUESSELER
Floating Clouds, the focal point of this polymer clay pendant, evoke the painterly technique associated with plein-air art.

SARAJANE HELM
Henna-ink Hands replicates, in polymer clay, the flowing patterns that characterize an ancient decorative art form that is still practiced in parts of India.

LEFT ANN DILLON
Klimt-Inspired colors and patterns come together in this handsome polymer clay pin. PHOTO BY ARTIST

CYNTHIA TOOPS AND DAN ADAMS
Aboriginal Motifs were referenced by the artists who created this evocative polymer clay necklace. PHOTO BY ROGER SCHREIBER

STONE, BONE, AND WOOD
Traditions

Imitating nature's textures presents exciting challenges to polymer clay artists. This chapter offers examples in three categories: suggesting the look of polished stone by capturing in clay the play of light on a stone's surface; simulating in clay the bone-decoration techniques of skilled scrimshaw carvers; and emulating in clay the different grain patterns and colors of parquetry and other fine wood objects.

We'll start with stone; emulating it brings us in contact with folklore passed down through the centuries in many cultures. The ancient Greeks, for example, believed that amethyst had the power to protect the wearer from drunkenness. Even today, "rock hounds" search for certain stones to turn into good-luck amulets. As a child, I thought stones looked like plain old rocks. But when my grandfather made the art of lapidary his serious retirement hobby—carefully cutting and polishing stones and turning them into beautiful pieces of jewelry—I realized how wrong I had been. Now, his treasures have become yet another source of inspiration for my eclectic projects. Those who wish to specialize in this popular category will find many books and videos on the market that are devoted exclusively to instructing techniques for imitating stones and gemstones in polymer clay. Here, we touch on one of the most intriguing approaches to copying stones: the chatoyant techniques.

J. M. SYRON AND BONNIE BISHOFF
Pedestal End Table features cherrywood with polymer clay veneers. PHOTO BY DEAN POWELL

CHATOYANT STONE TECHNIQUES

DERIVED FROM the French verb *chatoyer,* "to shine like a cat's eye," chatoyant is the term that describes light reflecting off of a surface, as in the look of a tiger's-eye stone. Among polymer clay artists, Karen Lewis first used the word to describe creations made by Pier Voulkos, who began working with the metallic Premo! clay, a polymer clay laden with mica particles. Soon, others also saw the potential of this new clay and the distinct qualities offered by mica combined with translucent clay. When Mike Buesseler beta tested the same clay, he noticed its variations of

color, and achieved amazing results by stacking slices of clay cut from a conditioned slab at odd angles to create unusual beads.

Just prior to Pier's retirement, I was fortunate to be able to take one of her classes, where I learned chatoyant methods, or what she calls her "invisible cane" techniques, demonstrated here with her permission. Only when you try them for yourself will you appreciate them fully, because photographs simply cannot convey the sense of depth and movement seen when light catches polymer clay objects like these.

JUDY BELCHER
My attempt at mica shift resulted in these beads, the round ones showing the concentric circular shapes that suggest cat's-eye, as does the Voulkos box chatoyant pattern below.

MIKE BUESSELER
"Mica shift," a term that's used interchangeably with *chatoyant,* describes the unique illusory effect produced by the mixture of mica particles with translucent clay, as shown in the subtle gradations of color that distinguish this handsome pendant.

RIGHT **PIER VOULKOS**
A brightly colored lidded box with a fanciful handle owes its added appeal to what the artist calls "invisible canes," her term for the chatoyant effect of a subtle pattern that seems to reflect light from within when viewed from different angles. PHOTO BY GEORGE POST

Chatoyant Checkerboard and Jellyroll Canes

SUPPLIES

metallic clay
sharp blade
acrylic rod
pasta machine

To achieve any chatoyant effect, the one color of metallic clay must be rolled through the pasta machine many times to line up all the mica particles. Think of the mica particles as tiny mirrors. When the clay comes out of the package, the "mirrors" are scattered within the clay. As you roll it through the pasta machine over and over, all the "mirrors" reposition themselves, side-by-side and flat, with the reflective side up. If you look down at the top of the sheet of clay, the surface is very shiny. If you look at the side view of all those stacked-up "mirrors," there will be no reflective surface. If you cut the stacks of "mirrors" diagonally, there will be some reflective qualities, but not as bright as the top. Therefore, within one sheet of clay there are many different values of the same "color." The key to caning with metallic clays is to find each value within a sheet or slab of clay.

❶ After conditioning five sheets of clay on the thickness setting of your pasta machine, roll them together with an acrylic rod to form a single slab, and cut into even slices, using a Marxit or ruler to space the slices evenly.

❷ Roll a sheet of well-conditioned clay the same height and length of the slices. Lay the slices on top of the sheet, lined up in the same direction, and adhere gently with your acrylic rod, forcing out any air while being careful not to bruise the clay or disturb the mica particles.

3 Cut the sheet formed earlier into five equal increments and stack, making sure that the colors alternate in color value. After marking the top of the stack with a Marxit or ruler, cut to form a series of striped slices of the same width.

4 Alternate the slices by flipping every other one over to form a checkerboard pattern.

5 Completed Chatoyant Checkerboard Cane. While not readily obvious in the photo, slices of the checkerboard cane will show varying highlights when turned in different directions, thanks to the mica-shift quality of this technique. Slices such as these are now ready to be applied to any project of your choice.

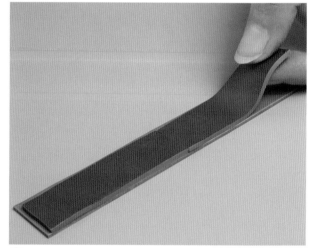

6 Repeat Steps 1 and 2. This image shows the slices from Step 1 being laid out on top of the sheet from Step 2. Check the side view of your sheets to make sure you have a shiny layer and a dull layer.

7 Using a blade, bevel one end of the sheet slightly to allow ease in forming the jellyroll. Beginning with the beveled end, roll the sheet up tightly.

8 Completed Chatoyant Jellyroll Cane. When you cut the roll into slices for your project, you may be inclined to compress the canes to be sure the pieces stick together, but be careful; pressure may cause the mica particles to scatter and diminish the effect.

Added Depth. The caning effect is lovely as is, but is more impressive when applied to sheets of clay and run through the pasta machine. To create a wonderful feeling of depth, place cane slices randomly on a sheet of clay and gently flatten with an acrylic rod. The depth becomes more apparent with each additional layer of slices.

SUPPLIES

metallic polymer clay
water spritzer
rubber stamp
sharp blade
pasta machine
sandpaper

DEMONSTRATION

Chatoyant Stamped Images

Rubber stamps or texture sheets can make a lovely chatoyant effect with the metallic clays. Remembering the mirror example, think about the many "colors" that can be achieved by all the different angles created by the surface of a rubber stamp.

1 Prepare a sheet of well-conditioned clay approximately the size of your chosen rubber stamp. Mist the stamp and press it firmly into the clay.

2 Because the rubber stamp (left) has the deeply cut lines required for stamping clay, the floral pattern has been clearly impressed on the clay sheet (right).

3 With a very sharp blade, shave all the raised portions of the clay to reveal the chatoyant image. Roll through the pasta machine to smooth the surface. Even the shavings have a nice chatoyant effect; use them to decorate other sheets of clay.

Completed Chatoyant Stamped Images: These examples show how such patterns seem to pop out even further when smoothed with wet/dry sandpaper of 600, 800, or 1000 grit, and polished on a buffing wheel.

BONE SIMULATIONS

FOR THOUSANDS OF YEARS, artisans have been fashioning both practical and decorative items out of animal bones. Ivory elephant tusks have been carved into treasured weapons, jewelry, and varied objets d'art. Bird bones, animal teeth, claws, and antlers have also been transformed into beads for jewelry or carved into buttons for fine clothing. Scrimshaw—the art of carving and etching baleen, a whale ivory—is a truly original American folk art developed by sailors on long voyages aboard whaling ships. By creating a faux ivory, scrimshaw can be replicated convincingly in polymer clay.

FAUX SCRIMSHAW

To imitate scrimshaw in polymer clay, mix two parts translucent clay with one part white clay. Roll out a sheet of the mixed clay on the thickest setting of your pasta machine, and cut out the shape of the finished piece you have in mind. If you bake the clay for about ten minutes, it will be easy to etch a design into it; but first, sketch your design on the baked clay with a soft lead pencil. Then, with a needle, go over your sketch, making a series of holes along the whole design. The closer the holes, the darker the lines appear. Use black acrylic paint to enhance the scratched and dotted areas, and wipe off any excess paint with a paper towel. Buff with a soft cloth to give the piece an ivorylike glow.

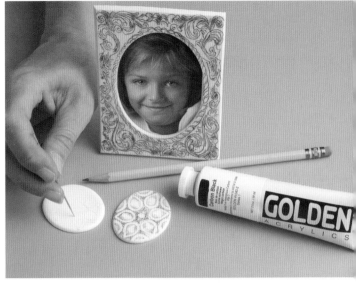

JUDY BELCHER
Faux Scrimshaw Frame and Pin. To guide my frame design, I pressed a rubber stamp lightly into the clay prior to baking. After baking, I scratched the image with the tip of a craft knife. For the pin, I covered a piece of clay with plastic wrap prior to cutting, then used an oval cutter. By doing so, the plastic wrap caused the edges of the pin to be beveled as the cutter was pressed into the clay. After penciling the design on the pin, I used the traditional scrimshaw dot technique described at left to complete the piece.

KIM AND KATHERINE MCCLELLAND
This piece by contemporary scrimshaw artisans was created on bone using carving and etching methods originated by New England whalers centuries ago. PHOTO BY JERRY ANTHONY

WOOD SIMULATIONS

I BECAME INTERESTED in the ancient craft of wood-turning unexpectedly when Jacqueline Lee, a dear friend and fine polymer clay artist, called to see if I had any spare canes lying around (of course I did). She asked me to bake a few and send them to a close friend of hers who was doing research for a book about polymer clay designs. I mailed them off, and a week later, was surprised to receive many delightful tops turned from my polymer clay canes and fitted with handles. Only then did I realize that the person turning my canes on his wood lathe was Kip Christensen, Ph.D., an instructor of industrial design at Brigham Young University and the author of many wood-turning books.

ABOVE **JUDY BELCHER AND KIP CHRISTENSEN**
My polymer clay canes were transformed on Kip Christensen's wood lathe into these wonderful tops, measuring about two inches in diameter by an inch thick, fitted with wooden and plastic handles.
PHOTO BY DON DAFOE

RIGHT **KIP CHRISTENSEN AND JUDY BELCHER**
Created by master wood-turner Kip Christensen for his *Container* series, this handsome example is made of box elder burl and pink ivory wood, topped by my polymer clay to embellish the lid—another successful marriage of the two materials. PHOTO BY DON DAFOE

ABOVE CRAIG NUTT
By an acclaimed craftsman, *Green Asparagus Table with Drawers* is oil on carved wood. Whether expressed as furniture or sculpture, vegetables provide Craig Nutt with a visual, metaphorically rich, and evocative vocabulary. PHOTO BY RICKEY YANAURA

LEFT LINDLY HAUNANI
This artist shares furniture maker Craig Nutt's sense of whimsy in her vegetable work *Asparagus Shrines.*

INTARSIA

The age-old mosaic technique of intarsia—decorating woodwork with inlays of precious stones, gold, and ivory—reached its peak of artistry in Renaissance Italy in the form of marquetry, in which small pieces of wood veneer were inlaid in a larger wood surface, producing striking pictorial effects. Parquetry, a variation on the technique, refers to geometrically patterned wood pieces fashioned together as in flooring. It was the geometric nature of parquetry that especially piqued my interest when researching wood for this chapter. I studied different types of wood and saw how the grains vary from tight to loose, straight, wavy, or knotty, and how subtle variances of color occur within a species. Obviously, those qualities offer clay artists a rich range of design and palette choices in simulating parquetry, as shown in the next project.

DEMONSTRATION Parquetry Box and Pin

SUPPLIES

polymer clays: brown, white, red, black; metallic gold and copper

sharp blade

Precise-a-Slice

acrylic rod

pasta machine

craft knife

quilter's triangle

Contact paper

liquid polymer clay

wood box with lid

parchment paper

While the simulated wood inlays created here are for a box and a pin, the technique can be applied to a host of other items. Imagine what a charming addition a parquetry floor imitated in clay would be to any child's dollhouse. Or you might transform a plain wood tray into a fine, faux-parquetry serving piece. The options are limitless.

1 Construct four distinctly different canes to give the final project interesting color contrasts. Simulate the varying wood colors of maple, oak, walnut, and cherry by using differing mixes of brown, white, red, and black clays. Add liberal parts of metallic gold and copper clays to each blend, to give the "woods" a nice glow. Prepare at least four different hues of each wood.

2 Roll out sheets of each of the four colors of clay. Within each color group, vary the thickness of each sheet. Here, the "oak" sheets are combined.

3 Roll the combined sheet through your pasta machine at its thickest setting. Cut the sheet in half, stack the two, and roll through the machine again on the thickest setting. You may need to do this step several times if your chosen wood has a tight grain.

4 Cut the sheet into four uneven sections.

5 Begin to roll a few of the sections into a partial jellyroll cane.

6 Cut each section in half lengthwise to create eight small sheets. Because oak has distinctive graining, I added very thin sheets of a dark brown to accentuate the grain. Combine all the sheets randomly, even messily. Layer each sheet, turning some over and letting some hang over the edge.

7 Compress the cane into a rectangle, using your hands, the tabletop, and an acrylic rod. Try to force waves in the cane to simulate the wood grain.

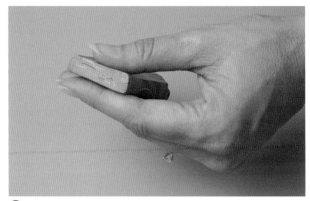

8 When the cane is fully compressed, square up the edges with an acrylic rod. The cane should now look like this.

9 The finished canes (from left): walnut, cherry, maple, oak, with thin sheets of each (foreground).

10 Cut very thin slices, enough to cover a base sheet completely. Using a Precise-a-Slice will produce slices of the same thickness. Line slices up to resemble plank flooring, butting their edges. Work in long rows, using your blade to press them together. Be sure not to trap air under the slices, as the final sheet will be very thin and will show every air pocket.

11 With an acrylic rod, roll the cane slices into the sheet, then roll the sheet through your pasta machine with the wood grain perpendicular to the rollers to elongate the grains, not widen them. Continue rolling at thinner settings. Bake the sheets for 25 minutes at 275 degrees. While still warm, place the sheets between two pieces of parchment paper and weigh them down with a heavy object to flatten. Let them cool.

12 Use the noodle-cutting attachment that may have come with your pasta machine to cut even strips of wood. A craft knife or paper cutter works as well, but takes much longer.

⓭ On the sticky side of clear Contact paper, lay out your strips of "wood." A simple geometric pattern works well with this technique, planned first on paper. Then measure and cut the wood strips needed.

⓮ A quilter's triangle aids in making 45-degree and 90-degree cuts. Form your design temporarily on another piece of Contact paper to be sure the edges and angles fit together nicely. Then you'll lift each piece from the paper to create your design on the surface chosen for the finished piece.

JUDY BELCHER
Completed Parquetry Box and Pin. The design was finalized and transferred to a wooden box coated with liquid clay, then baked and buffed with a soft cloth. All sides of the box, including the bottom, are now covered in polymer clay. The coordinated piece, the polymer clay pin, looks so much like wood that it's a true trompe-l'oeil delight when worn on the lapel.

Stone, Bone, and Wood Traditions in Polymer Clay

CYNTHIA TOOPS
Gradations: From her "Rolodex" series, this bracelet's creamy colors are based on the subtle gradations of tone characteristic of real ivory bangles.
PHOTO BY ROGER SCHREIBER

MARCIA LASKA
Faux Alabaster: The aesthetic and functional qualities of polymer clay come together in this lovely, useful, faux-alabaster rice bowl with matching chopsticks. PHOTO BY RICK LEE

ROBERT WILEY
Pretend Parquetry:
With its coloration faithful to wood tones and its pattern precisely cut and assembled, this polymer clay neckpiece simulates parquetry realistically.
PHOTO BY RICK WELLS

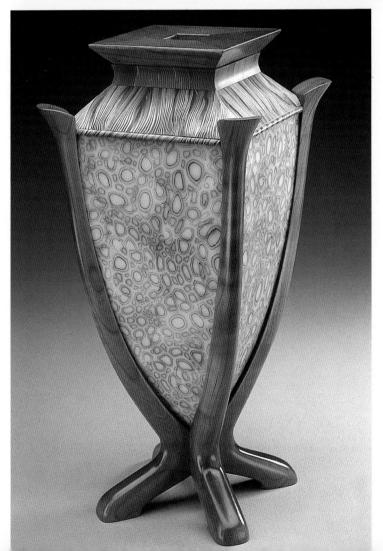

J. M. SYRON AND BONNIE BISHOFF
Mermaid Vessel combines a real cherrywood frame with polymer clay veneers that are stylized renditions of burled and grainy woods. PHOTO BY DEAN POWELL

MONA KISSEL
Slices Necklace:
Smartly combined with gold fittings, these polymer clay beads, in graduated sizes, bear the unmistakable texture of wood grain.
PHOTO BY ARTIST

CATHY JOHNSTON
Bamboolike Bangles:
In a perfect simulation of bamboo, these polymer clay bangles reflect the color, shape, and simple elegance of nature's original.

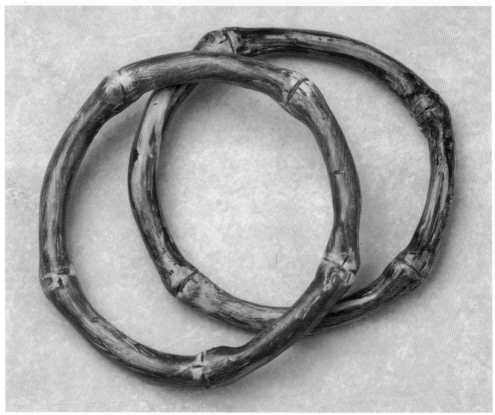

JUDY BELCHER

Ensemble: This chatoyant bracelet, pendant, and earrings set is based on the same caning technique, but with a twist. The cane is formed into a shell shape and sliced to reveal the chatoyant effect. The pendant's snake chain is sterling silver, as are the other fittings, and accented with blue topaz gemstones.

MAJ-BRITT CAWTHON

Simulated Bone: Sophisticated design and expertise in handling polymer clay give this faux-bone necklace its great eye-appeal.

PHOTO BY MADDOG STUDIO

IRENE YURKEWYCH
Vessel, although made entirely of only one color polymer clay, shows the artist's skillful use of the mica-shift technique to produce many lively tonal variations.
PHOTO BY ARTIST

ABOVE **JUDY BELCHER**
Elegant bracelets using chatoyant caning techniques are complemented with sterling silver links.

RIGHT **GAIL RITCHEY**
Faux Shell: Covering the body of this glass piece with a classic design created in polymer clay turns an ordinary vase into a faux-shell work of art.

ABOVE JANIS HOLLER
Hummer Bone: This interesting wall piece features a sculpted hummingbird and flowers in polymer clay, accented with stones and a bone. PHOTO BY ARTIST

LEFT HEIDI KUMMLI
Strong Heart is by an award-winning beading artist who turns her talents to combining beads with a polymer clay piece by Janis Holler to create this extraordinary necklace. PHOTO BY ARTIST

SCULPTURE AND CERAMICS
Traditions

Sculpture records the human experience in a three-dimensional way and, along with ceramics created through the ages, offers polymer clay artists a world of inspiration.

The art of sculpture began when the first Homo sapiens chipped away at a stone or tree to make a hunting tool, a figural carving, or a religious icon. In subsequent millennia, sculpture went on to record historical events. For example, what might appear as ornamental carvings on the entrance to a Mayan tomb actually tells the story of the ruler buried within. The focus of Japanese netsuke sculpture, on the other hand, was to make the world a more beautiful place. Even completely functional objects such as money pouches or tobacco pouches had elegantly carved toggles that are now highly collectible works of art. The Greeks perfected techniques to carve stone and marble and to cast bronze, allowing them greater detail in recording important people and events and in decorating buildings to please the gods.

The art of ceramics probably began the first time a human being scooped up wet dirt, formed it into a shape resembling cupped hands, and, with the aid of fire, turned it into a permanent vessel to hold water. Indeed, all early ceramics were earthen clay pressed by hand and used to contain items. Then potters devised the coiling method, as depicted in Egyptian tomb paintings. Throwing pots on a wheel followed centuries later, but only in the eighteenth century was mechanical power added, allowing for controlled speed and ease of throwing a pot.

MAUREEN CARLSON
The Helper: Polymer clay face, arms, and boots are
expertly sculpted in this engaging figure.

SCULPTURE

NOT BEING A SCULPTOR, I recruited the help of Leslie Blackford, a wonderfully talented artist from Kentucky. She often uses Indian symbols to decorate the forms that she sculpts, and although she isn't classically trained, her sculptures evoke an organic, or tribal, feeling.

Leslie began her journey with polymer clay by attempting to portray realistic faces. She would sculpt each feature separately, and then apply all the facial parts to the form of a head. Not satisfied with the outcome, she began modifying her approach.

Instead of aiming for very realistically rendered portraits, she would suggest features in a freer, more stylized way, using only a simple carved line for a mouth or a small bump of clay for a nose. That looser expression then led her to explore other subject matter, resulting in the creation of a wonderful array of modern "artifacts" inspired by the history of the land around her. This chapter's first demonstration is based on her method of sculpting from one solid piece of clay and prodding it into an amazing work of art.

LESLIE BLACKFORD
A stylized portrait sculpted in polymer clay and adorned with disparate objects and symbols all adds up to an intriguing mixed message conveyed in mixed media.

JACQUELINE LEE
This polymer clay necklace features the replica of a Mayan chieftain. It was made from a mold of an actual fragment found in a tomb having narrative decoration related to the deceased who lay within.

NORA JEAN GATINE
Deliciously realistic, these polymer clay mini hors d'oeuvres delight the eye as they whet the appetite. Miniature foods were first sculpted in polymer clay by artists who found their niche making adornments for dollhouses, furthering the tradition started by the doll makers who pioneered using the material to construct the dolls.

SUPPLIES

polymer clays: white, yellow, brown, green

needle tool

clay-shaping tools

sharp blade

glass beads

optional add-ons

DEMONSTRATION # Triangle Horse

Starting with a simple form like a triangle and a little imagination, you can create numerous designs that build on this basic technique. We begin with an animal head that has an organic, or primitive, look. To establish that aura, use a mixture of clays—mostly white with pinches of others—to produce a "dirty ivory" tone. Form the clay into the general shape of a horse's head, and finish it off with a few carvings and glass beads for eyes. While any brand of clay may be used, I recommend Kato Polyclay because its density allows handling the piece as you work, without distorting the shape. Once you've sculpted the basic head, add expression and touches to make it your own. You might apply a stain, paint, or patina medium to create a more dramatic effect. Or perhaps you want your horse to have a more realistic look? If so, add a mane, whiskers, and teeth, which will change the head's overall appearance completely, as will other accents that you may dream up to give the head your own personal stamp.

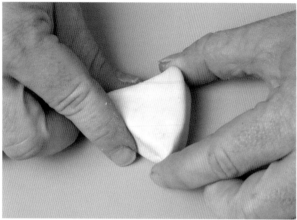

1 After mixing white clay with pinches of yellow, brown, and green to give it a slightly "dirty-ivory" tone, form the clay into a triangle.

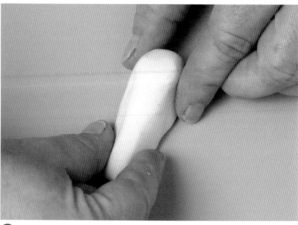

2 Pull one end of the triangle slightly to elongate the head shape. Soften and round the corners and edges.

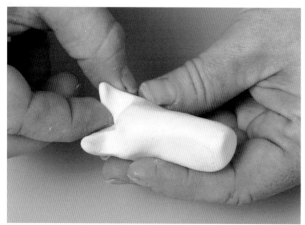

3 Pinch the top two corners upward for the ears, then sculpt and smooth them into the desired position. Keeping the ears pointed straight up helps maintain the appearance of a horse. Square up the nose end by gently pressing the point into your work surface.

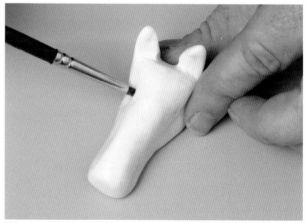

4 With a pointed clay shaper (this one by Forsline) make evenly spaced impressions where you wish to place the eyes. Use your fingers to smooth and even out the head shape.

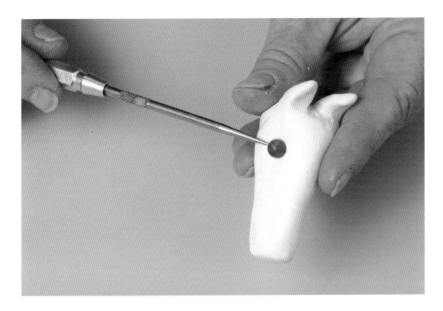

5 Place a glass bead on the tip of a needle tool and impress it into place for one eye. Press slightly to secure the bead. Slide the needle tool out, making sure the holes of the bead are not visible, and repeat the procedure for the other eye. The smooth shine of glass gives depth to the eyes and makes them look more realistic.

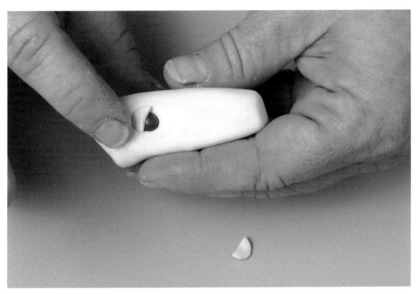

6 Start the eyelid by making a pea-sized ball of clay. Press it against your work surface into a flattened circle, then cut it in half. The lid position helps determine the expression and mood of the horse, so place the lid at different angles to find the one you like best.

TIP

An eyelid straight across creates a shallow, lost, or puzzled expression. Half-closed lids give the character a sleepy, lazy, or carefree appearance. When lids are directed toward the nose, the face takes on a dark, mischievous, or angry look. Eyelids angled away from the nose suggest a sweet, innocent, or even bashful personality.

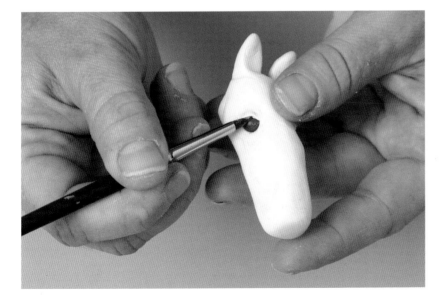

7 Use light pressure on a clay shaper to set the lid securely in place in the position you've decided on. Here, the straight edge overlaps the top of the bead slightly. Repeat the procedure for the other lid.

8 If you choose to make a mane, roll out a thin snake of clay, cut it into about five pieces, join them at one end, and attach to the horse's head.

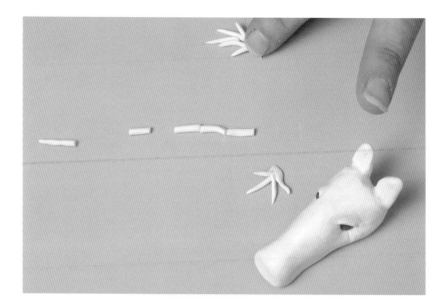

9 For nostrils, use your needle tool to make two holes at the end of the nose. They should be deep enough to look realistic.

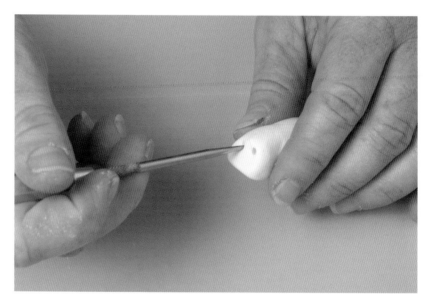

10 Use your needle tool to draw a thin, shallow line for the mouth.

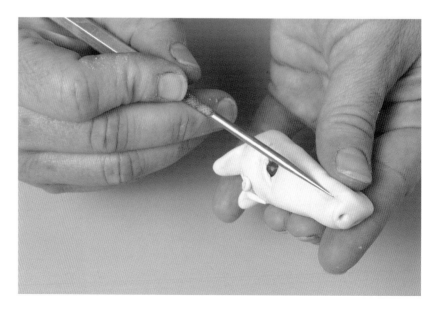

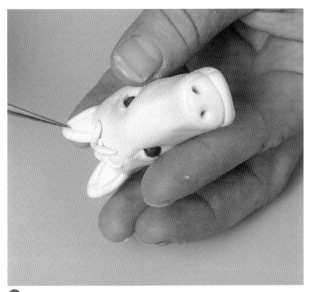

11 Use your needle tool to draw in other details, such as the outline of the ears.

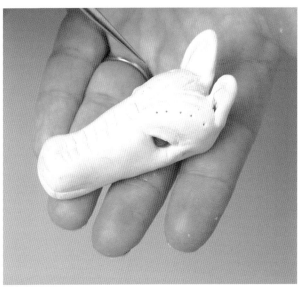

12 To create a primitive look, leave off the mane and carve or texture decorative elements.

LESLIE BLACKFORD
Completed Triangle Horse: Along with the horse head demonstrated (right), variations include other animal heads and a pendant, all based on the same sculpture techniques.

WHILE RESEARCHING sculpture and working with sculpting mediums, I found it fascinating that most of the techniques used in enhancing the surface of polymer clay found their roots in ceramic techniques. Those techniques may be divided into four categories: altering the clay body itself; using slip, a liquid form of clay; using glazes and different firing techniques; and using printed decorations. To demonstrate those methods, I've chosen to apply clay to a four-inch-square white ceramic tile, but the same techniques can be used on a glass vase or other surfaces to replicate actual ceramic. With your imagination as the added ingredient, polymer clay will reward you with a rich array of beautiful faux-ceramic works of art.

ALTERING THE CLAY BODY

Adding texture to a piece for visual interest can be accomplished with commercially made texture sheets, rubber stamps, various tools, found objects, and forms from nature. To keep a texturing device from sticking to the clay, mist it with water or cornstarch before applying it. Using cutters, decorative scissors, or simply tearing an earthen-clay sheet will also contribute interesting surface effects, as will thin sheets of clay or slices of canework added for decoration.

When adhering adornments to the clay, to avoid trapping air beneath, start at one end and press gently as you work across the additional element. Then roll the decoration flat into the surface of the clay. Thin slices of a cane can add elements of design as a focal point. Use a Marxit to make precise slices of equal thickness. Roll the slices in all directions with an acrylic rod to assure good adherence and decrease the likelihood of air being trapped beneath.

ABOVE BRIAN VAN NOSTRAND
Ceramists use many methods, as do polymer artists, to impress decoration in the surface of their clay. This handsome vase is part of a series that appeared in *Ceramics Monthly* featuring this artisan's impressive (in both senses) ceramic work.
PHOTO BY CRAIG JAY CLARK

RIGHT Pictured are clay stamps of hobo symbols that I made from scrap clay (left); example of textured sheet (center); a texture sheet from the Lisa Pavelka collection (right); and two wooden texturing rollers made by Sue Kelsey.

Mishima and Decorative Layers

Inlaying by incising patterns into earthen clay or applying decorative layers of earthen clay to a piece are methods that have been known to potters for thousands of years. They are versatile means of adding distinctive patterns or colors into the body of the piece. Mishima is a method of Korean origin, whereby incised lines are filled with a contrasting color of clay. Then the surface is scraped so that only the carved lines remain filled with inserted clay.

SUPPLIES

4"-square white ceramic tile

Skinner Blends (see p. 19): black-to-white, purple-to-white

canes: brightly colored flowers, green leaves

sharp blade

acrylic rod

V-shaped linoleum cutter

1 On a white ceramic tile, apply a 3"-x-3" sheet of black-to-white Skinner Blend that has been rolled on the thickest setting of your pasta machine. To avoid trapping air beneath the clay sheet, start at one edge and roll the clay carefully over the ceramic tile, smoothing as you go. Slice small pockets of air with a sharp blade, then mend the hole by blending gently with your finger. Place several flower and leaf slices, and then flatten them with your acrylic rod. Bake the clay on the ceramic tile for 10 minutes at 275 degrees, which will partially cure the clay and make it easier to carve.

2 To add mishima technique to the piece, carve a decorative design, being careful not to slice all the way through the clay. Here, my choice is a decorative design of my daughter's initials.

3 To complete the mishima accent, cut a strip of your purple-to-white Skinner Blend sheet and roll it into a thin snake that will fit neatly into the carved incision.

4 Scrape off the excess clay to reveal a smooth surface design. Bake the entire piece again for 20 minutes at 275 degrees.

JUDY BELCHER
Completed Mishima and Decorative Layers: Adorning a plain ceramic tile with polymer clay can produce a personalized, one-of-a-kind gift.

SPRIGGING

Applying raised decorations to pottery is a technique that's synonymous with the Wedgwood company's white relief designs on blue jasperware. A fine way to copy that look is by adding baked-clay embellishments to a raw piece of clay with super glue. Lisa Pavelka markets a poly bonder that works well and can withstand baking temperatures. To preserve details of the element being added, one way is to bake the molded piece and then add it to the object. If you choose this method, adhere the element to the piece with liquid clay, but use a dab of poly bonder to hold it in place during the baking process.

USING SLIP

When working with polymer clay, using liquid polymer clay to decorate a surface is like using slip, or liquid earthen clay, in ceramics to add patterns and colors to a base piece. Ceramists often employ stencils to aid in designing open patterns. A variation on the technique is slip trailing. A thick slip is placed in a bottle with a nozzle. When squeezed, a thick line of slip creates a slightly raised texture. Easily emulated by polymer clay artists, if the surface you are decorating is vertical, apply the liquid clay to a surface that is hot from the oven. It will partially bake when applied and not run down the piece.

Sprigging: To give my example the appearance of Wedgwood, I applied the white raised pattern to a sheet of blue clay. I began with a rubber stamp dusted with cornstarch, then rolled out a sheet of white clay on my pasta machine and placed it on the rubber stamp. After dusting the back of the clay with more cornstarch, I embedded it into the stamp, then bent the stamp to release the design.

Slip Trailing: Using a container with a pointed nozzle, I filled it with a teaspoon of pearl pigment mixed with two ounces of liquid clay, then squeezed out a simple design of lines, curves, dots, and squiggles.

SGRAFFITO

The word *sgraffito,* from the Italian word for scratch, refers to the incised design cut through a layer of colored slip to reveal the color of the body beneath. To simulate the look of sgraffito, use contrasting colors of polymer clays and inks.

GLAZING AND FIRING

Majolica, resist, and raku are three glazing and firing ceramic techniques that adapt well to polymer clay projects. Majolica, developed by Moorish craftsmen on the island of Majorca, features bold colors painted over an unfired dry surface treated with opaque tin or lead glazes that melt into the colors when fired. To replicate in polymer clay, apply canes, paint, or inks to the surface to create a richly colored design. Resist techniques, using wax paper and latex, can be copied by substituting Repel Gel applied to polymer clay and then baked to act as a resist for further additions of tinted liquid clay or inks. Finally, raku (Japanese for "enjoyment") combines a clay body, glazes, and firing into thick earthenware usually of irregular shape and texture. To simulate in polymer clay, the projects that follow present two versions of raku.

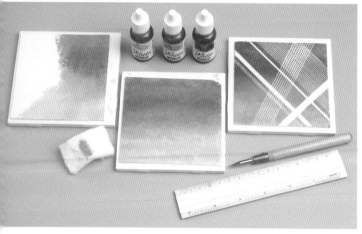

Sgraffito: To simulate this incised method, I applied three inks on a sheet of baked white clay. Then, with a needle tool and ruler, I scratched off the colorful surface in geometric patterns to reveal the base clay.

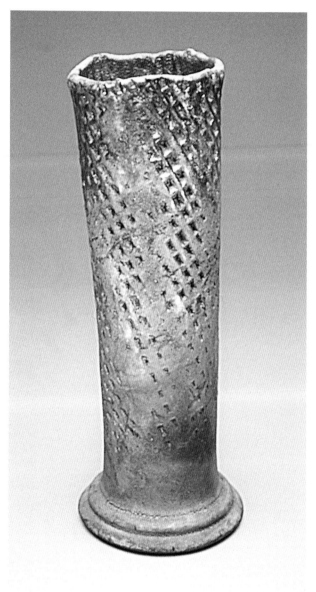

JOSEPH LUNG
This high-fired sgraffito porcelain plate offers a fine example of an elegant design technique employed by a master ceramist.
PHOTO BY CHUCK WYROSTOCK

DIANA PITTIS
A beautiful example of raku, this graceful vase is by a skilled ceramist whose technique is faithful to a classic art form dating back to the sixteenth century. PHOTO BY MIKE KELLER

DEMONSTRATION Metallic Raku

SUPPLIES

black polymer clay

60-grit sandpaper

metallic pigment powders: bronze, blue, bright gold, turquoise, red

matte varnish

I applied a 4"-×-4" sheet of black clay over a white ceramic tile, but you might choose to cover a vase or other ceramic surface with black clay or make beads for a bracelet using this technique. If possible, it's helpful to look at real raku for inspiration as you follow these steps.

① Prior to baking, texture the surface of the clay with 60-grit sandpaper. Press the sandpaper firmly and randomly to achieve the appearance of a clay body heavy with grog—that is, hard-fired clay that has been crushed or ground to particles of various sizes and incorporated into the body of the clay.

② After baking the piece according to the clay manufacturer's directions, sprinkle metallic pigment powders randomly from their little jars. Here, bronze and blue were applied first, but the muddy tone will be enlivened when the next colors are added.

JUDY BELCHER
Completed Metallic Raku: For a protected finish, seal the powders with a coat of matte varnish that is suitable for use on polymer clay.

Crackle Raku

SUPPLIES
white polymer clay
sheet of heavy white paper
acrylic rod
acrylic paints: black, gray
protective glove
paper towel
toothbrush
gloss varnish

I used a 4"-×-4" sheet of white clay over a white ceramic tile, but, as with the previous project, you might choose to cover a vase or other object with white clay—or, better yet, combine the two techniques for a lovely contrasting piece.

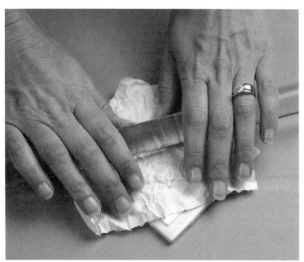

1 Crumple up a piece of heavy white paper, then smooth it so it lies flat while retaining its creases. Roll the paper into the clay with an acrylic rod. This step may have to be repeated several times to impress the desired crinkled texture.

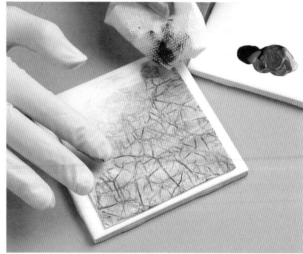

2 Bake according to the clay manufacturer's directions. Use a gloved hand to apply a mixture of black and gray acrylic paint. With a paper towel, work the paint into all the crevices. Wipe off any excess paint.

To complete crackle raku, using a toothbrush loaded with a mixture of the paints, spatter some additional paint randomly across the piece. Brush on several coats of a high- gloss varnish.

JUDY BELCHER
Real raku and simulated can look so alike, it may be hard to tell them apart. Here, my polymer clay vase, combining metallic and crackle raku techniques, drew inspiration from a ceramic raku box that I purchased several years ago.

PRINTING ON CERAMICS is not a new technique. Medieval floor tiles were made with the intaglio printing method to produce repeating patterns. Further developments in transferring images revolutionized mass-produced ceramics. Among the printing methods used today to decorate ceramics are stencils, monoprinting, decals, and silk-screening.

Using a stencil to print on polymer clay is an easy way to get consistent and repeating images. With numerous decorative stencils on the market, the range of choices for polymer clay artists is endless.

Monoprinting lets us experiment with line drawings that can then be transferred to clay by duplicating the image with a toner-based copier and burnishing the paper against the raw clay.

Printed transfers are epitomized by the willow pattern in dinnerware and are also used for application to other mass-produced pottery of all sorts. For transferring images to polymer clay, one new product is a waterslide transfer. The image need only be cut out, brushed lightly with water and burnished against the clay, then baked accordingly.

Silk-screening is another method of decorating the surface of both ceramics and polymer clay. As its name suggests, in this printing method ink or paint is brushed through a fine screen of silk to create a design.

In these two examples of printed transfers, a waterslide decal is shown being printed on white polymer clay. A light mist of water applied to the back of the decal allows the paper backing to slide right off, leaving the image attached to the clay. In the foreground is a finished pin using a transferred image, framed in black clay, and embellished with flower-petal cane slices.

GWEN GIBSON
Crane Pendant is a beautiful example of a silk-screen design applied to polymer clay by an artist and teacher of her craft, who markets her own product line of pre-made silk screens that can be used over and over again to create all kinds of jewelry pieces. PHOTO BY ROBERT DIAMANTE

Sculpture and Ceramics Traditions in Polymer Clay

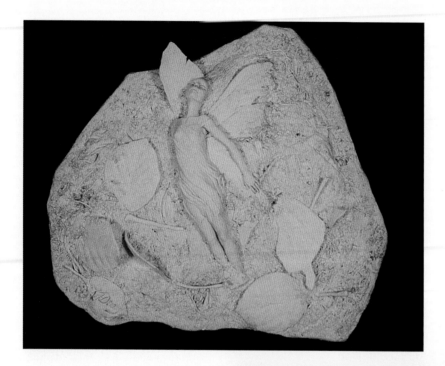

KATHERINE DEWEY
Travertine, inspired by the tradition of great statues emerging from rough-hewn marble, is aptly titled, even though its richly carved figure is of polymer clay, not stone. PHOTO BY ROLAND KRUEGER

SUSAN SAMITZ
Face Brooch is an excellent example of bas-relief sculpture rendered in polymer clay. The layering of fanciful adornments atop the head adds great interest to the profile. PHOTO BY MARC CORLISS

JEFFREY LLOYD DEVER
Crustacea is instantly recognizable as the work of a polymer clay artist whose highly innovative designs often incorporate flora, pods, and other stylized natural matter such as the seaform appendages on this vase. PHOTO BY GREGORY R. STALEY

OLIVIA ASH TURNER
Leaf Mask, by an exceptionally fine sculptor, reflects her sophisticated techniques transferred to polymer clay.

ABOVE OSCELYN A. ANDERSON

Nativity displays how this artist has honed the art of creating sculptures to a fine craft. Her sense of humor and attention to detail read clearly in all of her polymer clay work. PHOTO BY PAUL ELBO, PRS ASSOC.

RIGHT LYNDA STRUBLE

Two Fairies have such expressive faces, they seem about to come alive. PHOTO BY MARGO SEARLS-BEGY

ABOVE L. M. POLINKO
Sleeping Dragon, down to its claws and scales, is a precisely detailed polymer clay sculpture with an amusing, altogether original take on a fiercely funny creature.

LEFT SANDRA THOMAS OGLESBY
Carrier of the Light is painted polymer with cotton thread embedded in the scalp for hair and then also painted. A sweet face and animated stance add to the figure's charm. PHOTO BY ARTIST

DOROTHY GREYNOLDS
Bugs combines impressed and relief sculpting techniques with strong designs and colors, resulting in a trio of eye-catching polymer clay creations.

SARAJANE HELM

Mini Dinnerware is an assortment of charming, Wedgwood-inspired items replicated in polymer clay and sure to delight a dollhouse owner or other collector of miniatures.

VALERIE MURCHAKE WRIGHT

Faux-Raku Jewelry displays metallic and crackle techniques that complement each other in this polymer clay pair with its evocative yin-yang pattern on both bracelet and pin.

LAURA TABAKMAN
Locket Portrait is a striking example of raku technique applied to polymer clay and further enhanced with subtle coloration and highly imaginative abstract design. PHOTO BY ARTIST

ABOVE **JEAN COMPORT**
Fancy Face has smoothly sculpted and decorated features, impressed eyebrows, and a relief pattern on the hat, which all contribute to this engaging, many-method polymer clay pendant.

LEFT **DONNA KATO**
Carved Pendant brings simplicity and elegance together in a stylized floral expertly incised against a background of contrasting polymer clay color, turning that negative space into a dominant design element.

PARTICIPATING ARTISTS

ADAMS, DAN
Seattle, Washington
ANDERSON, OSCELYN A.
Takoma Park, Maryland

BECKER, CYNTHIA
Pueblo, Colorado
BELCHER, JUDY
St. Albans, West Virginia
BISHOFF, BONNIE
(with: see Syron)
Rockport, Massachusetts
BLACKFORD, LESLIE
Munfordville, Kentucky
BONHAM, MAGS
Bolton, Vermont
BRAMS, DEBORAH
Hull, Massachusetts
BUESSELER, MIKE
Great Falls, Montana
BUNDY, NANCY
(with: see Paris)
Pampano Beach, Florida

CARLSON, MAUREEN
Jordan, Minnesota
CAVENDER, KIM
St. Albans, West Virginia
CAWTHON, MAJ-BRITT
Lakewood, Colorado
CHRISTENSEN, KIP
Springville, Utah
COMPORT, JEAN
Royal Oak, Michigan
COZZI, LOUISE FISCHER
Brooklyn, New York

DEVER, JEFFREY LLOYD
Laurel, Maryland
DEWEY, KATHERINE
Maxwell, Texas
DILLON, ANN
Hancock, New Hampshire
DONALDSON, CONNIE
Lawrence, Pennsylvania
DUSTIN, KATHLEEN
Contoocook, New Hampshire

ECHEAGARAY, PATRICIA
Adamstown, Maryland

FOLLETT, LORIE
Sandy, Utah
FORD AND FORLANO
Philadelphia, Pennsylvania

FRANKENBERG, MARLA
Pittsburgh, Pennsylvania

GARNER, TAMMY
St. Albans, West Virginia
GATINE, NORA JEAN
San Francisco, California
GIBSON, GWEN
San Rafael, California
GLAZER, CAT
(with: see Lambertson)
Lewisburg, West Virginia
GRAHAM, DENISE
Pittsburgh, Pennsylvania
GREYNOLDS, DOROTHY
Waterford, Michigan
GROVE, MICHAEL AND
RUTH ANN
Berkeley, California

HAUNANI, LINDLY
Cabin John, Maryland
HELM, SARAJANE
Longmont, Colorado
HOLLER, JANIS
Berthoud, Colorado
HYDE, SUSAN
Bremerton, Washington

IVESTER, SUZANNE
Knoxville, Tennessee

JACKSON, DEBBIE
Columbus, Ohio
JIMISON, CARLA
Rexburg, Idaho
JOHNSTON, CATHY
Pasco, Washington

KATO, DONNA
Florissant, Colorado
KELSEY, SUE
Ypsilanti, Michigan
KISSEL, MONA
Martinsburg, West Virginia
KLEW (KAREN LEWIS)
Tehachapi, California
KORRINGA, KIM
Mountainview, California
KUMMLI, HEIDI
Nederland, Colorado
KUSKIN, JUDY
Seattle, Washington

LAMBERTSON, KEITH
(with: see Glazer)
Lewisburg, West Virginia
LASKA, MARCIA
Bartow, West Virginia
LEE, JACQUELINE
Springville, Utah
LEHMAN, JAMES
Akron, Ohio
LISKA, LAURA
Sonoma, California
LORING, EILEEN
Windsor, Colorado
LUFTIG, DIANE
Denver, Colorado
LUNG, JOSEPH
Spencer, West Virginia

MAGGIO, MAGGIE
Portland, Oregon
MCCAW, SANDRA
Alstead, New Hampshire
MCCLELLAND, KIM AND
KATHERINE
Galina, Ohio
MCCOMAS, DEBBIE
Huntington, West Virginia
MCGUIRE, BARBARA A.
Suwanee, Georgia
MIDGETT, STEVE
Franklin, North Carolina
MIKA, LAURIE
Encinitas, California
MILLS, LIBBY
Glastonbury, Connecticut
MITCHELL, ANN AND
KAREN
Altadena, California

NUTT, CRAIG
Kingston Springs, Tennessee

OGLESBY, SANDRA
THOMAS
DeLand, Florida
OSBAHR, NANCY
Fort Collins, Colorado

PARIS, BOB
(with: see Bundy)
Pompano Beach, Florida
PAVELKA, LISA
Las Vegas, Nevada
PITTIS, DIANA
Daniels, West Virginia

POLINKO, L. M.
Pittsburgh, Pennsylvania

RITCHEY, GAIL
Birmingham, Alabama
ROSS, MICHELLE
Sherman Oaks, California

SAMITZ, SUSAN
Putney, Vermont
SEYMOUR, AMY
Munfordville, Kentucky
SHRIVER, SARAH NELSON
San Rafael, California
SIMMONS, CAROL
Fort Collins, Colorado
SKINNER, JUDITH
Prescott, Arizona
SPERLING, BARBARA
Chatham, New Hampshire
STRUBLE, LYNDA
Southfield, Michigan
SYRON, J. M.
(with: see Bishoff)
Rockport, Massachusetts

TABAKMAN, LAURA
Pittsburgh, Pennsylvania
TINAPPLE, CYNTHIA
Worthington, Ohio
TOOPS, CYNTHIA
Seattle, Washington
TURNER, OLIVIA ASH
Scott Depot, West Virginia

VAN NOSTRAND, BRIAN
Hacker Valley, West Virginia
VILLANO, DIANE
East Haven, Connecticut
VOULKOS, PIER
Oakland, California

WALL, MARCIA
Dublin, Ohio
WILEY, ROBERT
Sugarland, Texas
WINTERS, ELISE
Haworth, New Jersey
WRIGHT, VALERIE
MURCHAKE
Columbus, Ohio

YURKEWYCH, IRENE
Parsippany, New York

Manufacturers of the various tools and materials mentioned in this book will be pleased to direct you to the retailers nearest you that carry their products. Also contact these resources with any questions you might have about their products.

AMERICAN ART CLAY COMPANY
6060 Guion Road
Indianapolis, IN 46254
(800) 374-1600
www.amaco.com
FIMO, FIMO Soft, FIMO Gel, metallic powders, bead rollers, pasta machine, ceramic tools

CLEARSNAP
P. O. Box 98
Anacortes, WA 98221
(888) 448-4862
www.clearsnap.com
Stylus Molding Mats, ColorBox, Ancient Page, Vivid Inks

GWEN GIBSON
216 Bayview Street
San Rafael, CA 94901
(415) 454-3246
www.gwengibson.com
silk screen

HEART IN HAND STUDIOS/LISA PAVELKA
9825 Tarzana Lane
Las Vegas, NV 89117
(877) 411-5472
www.heartinhandstudio.com
texture stamps, transfers, poly bonder

KEMPER ENTERPRISES
13595 12th Street
Chino, CA 91710
(909) 627-6191
www.kempertools.com
Kemper Klay Gun, Kemper shape cutters, ceramic tools

MONA LISA PRODUCTS/HOUSTON ART
P. O. Box 72
Grand Haven, MI 49417
(800) 828-0359
www.hofcraft.com
metal leafing, pulverized metal powders

POLYFORM PRODUCTS
1901 Estes Avenue
Elk Grove Village, IL 60007
(847) 427-0020
www.sculpey.com
Sculpey III, Premo! Sculpey, Translucent Liquid Sculpey (TLS)

PRAIRIE CRAFT COMPANY
P. O. Box 209
Florissant, CO 80816
(800) 779-0615
www.prairiecraft.com
Kato Polyclay, Kato Clear Liquid Medium, Repel Gel, NuBlade, Marxit, Forsline, Starr Clay Shapers, acrylic rod

RANGER CRAFTS
15 Park Road
Tinton Falls, NJ 07724
(732) 389-3535
www.rangerink.com
Adirondack Alcohol Inks, Perfect Pearls, UTEE, Suze Weinberg's Melting Pot

RUPERT, GIBBON & SPIDER/ JACQUARD PRODUCTS
P. O. Box 425
Healdsburg, CA 95448
(800) 442-0455
www.jacquardproducts.com
Piñata inks, Lumiere paints, Pearl-ex powders

RUST-OLEUM
11 Hawthorn Parkway
Vernon Hills, IL 60061
(800) 553-8444
www.rustoleum.com
Gloss Flecto Varathane

SUE KELSEY
4755 Merritt Road
Ypsilanti, MI 48197
skel@comcast.net
curved magnet, textured wooden rollers

VALKAT DESIGNS
P. O. Box 12563
Columbus, OH 43212
valkatdesigns@hotmail.com
Precise-a-Slice

MICHAEL AND RUTH ANN GROVE
Double Woman Pin personifies this creative couple's signature theme, whimsical figures fashioned in polymer clay.